LEADERSHIP SKILLS FOR
WOMEN IN MISSIONS

Time
Management

New Hope
Birmingham, Alabama

DEBBIE LLOYD

Published by:
New Hope
P.O. Box 12065
Birmingham, AL 35202-2065

Unless otherwise indicated, Bible quotations are from the *Holy Bible: New International Version* © 1978 by the International Bible Society. Used by permission of Zondervan Bible Publishers.

Verses marked KJV are from *The Holy Bible,* King James Version.

Verses marked NEB are from *The New English Bible.* © The Delegates of Oxford University Press and The Syndics of the Cambridge University Press 1961, 1970. Reprinted by permission.

Verses marked RSV are from *The Holy Bible,* Revised Standard Version copyright 1952 by the Division of Christian Education of the National Council of the Churches of Christ in the United States of America. Used by permission.

Verses marked TEV are from *Good News Bible,* Today's English Version. Used by permission of American Bible Society. Copyright 1976.

Verses marked TLB are from *The Living Bible,* copyright 1971 by Tyndale House Publishers, Wheaton, IL. Used by permission.

Poem by Michel Quoist from *Prayers,* copyright 1985, Sheed and Ward, Kansas City. Used by permission.

Dewey Decimal classification: 248:843

Subject Headings: CHRISTIAN LIFE—WOMEN
                  TIME MANAGEMENT

Series: Leadership Skills for Women in Missions

ISBN: 1-56309-102-X

N943116•0294•7.5M1

Church Study Course number 03-385

Contents

Dedication

To Rich and my children, who by their joyful presence remind me of the necessity of separating the important from the urgent.

Lord, I have time.

I have plenty of time.

All the time that You give me.

The years of my life,

The days of my years,

The hours of my days,

They are all mine.

Mine to fill, quietly, calmly,

But to fill completely, to the brim,

To offer them to You, that of their

insipid water

You make a rich wine as

You made once in Cana of Galilee.

Michel Quoist

Me, A Time Manager?

I have always thought I practiced good time-management skills. My clocks are set five minutes fast to help me be on time. I never sit down to watch TV unless I have something to do with my hands. I load the dishwasher and fold clothes while talking on the phone. I enjoy making lists of errands to run and tasks to be accomplished, planning my "strategy of attack" for the day, and successfully marking items off the list. I even read the newspaper and cut out coupons while riding in the car.

Then why did many of my closest friends laugh when they learned that I had been asked to write a book on time management? They know me too well and there are some things you just can't hide. I'm the one who sat in the labor room sewing buttons on the "coming home" outfit for our second child (in between the systematic twinges of pain). I'm the one whose Christmas tree always has a beautiful tree skirt showing because I wrap gifts just before the party on Christmas Eve, or those out-of-town relatives come on December 26. I'm the one who mails Christmas cards as Valentines. I'm the one who stays up most of the night before a retreat or program that I've known about for months . . . gathering supplies and preparing notes. And yes, I'm the one who arrives for lunch with my editor, of all people, 15 minutes late (I got lost, honestly).

Like my friends, you, too, must be wondering why I was chosen to write this book. I've asked the same question myself, but I think I've found an answer. Just after signing the contract, I heard a popular psychiatrist on a television talk show say, "I always write the book I need most." Apparently others knew how much I needed this book. It's not that I procrastinate, I just try to do too much. I'm not really unorganized, I just seem to work better under pressure. I'm over committed, not good at saying no, the mother of two preschoolers, and the wife of a pastor. I put off until the last minute, not in laziness, but quite the opposite, in busyness. And until recently, I have taken great pride in that busyness. If you can identify with me, then this book is for you.

Although I write as a stay-at-home mother, a role I am proud of, I have had experience in a variety of roles: single, full-time student; single student/part-time worker; single, full-time employee; married, part-time student/part-time employee; married, full-time student/part-time employee; married, full-time employee; mother, part-time student/part-time worker; mother, full-time student; mother, part-time employee; mother, full-time employee. (Wow! How many other combinations are there?)

I can identify with most of you in terms of managing an overly-committed schedule. So I invite you to walk with me as I learn the much needed lessons of prioritizing, dealing with interruptions, saying no and making deliberate choices about my use of time. Take time to do the learning activities so that you, too, can better grasp just how to "redeem your time" (Col. 4:5, Eph. 5:16 KJV), or in a more modern translation, "make the most of every opportunity" (NIV).

CHAPTER ONE

A Time for Everything?

*There is a time for everything, and a season
for every activity under heaven (Ecc. 3:1).*

While reading an article about time management in a popular women's magazine, I first began thinking about the subject. A time management expert was evaluating a TV celebrity's use of her time to help her squeeze a little more out of her day. The advisor made the usual suggestions about laying out your clothes the night before, planning errands to coordinate with other necessary stops, and making lists and schedules.

For some reason, the more I read, the more the article bothered me. I began to wonder, is this what time management is all about—moving hurriedly and systematically through the day, marking off accomplished tasks from one's list? It must mean more than collapsing into bed at the end of a day holding a crumpled paper filled with affirming check marks . . . marks that chant, "Well done, Busy Bee! Look at all you did today!" Maybe the hurting friend who called really needed more than the recipe. Maybe the secretary in your office needed to talk to someone about her family's shaky financial situation after her uninsured 16-year-old's auto accident.

Surely time management is more than mechanically squeezing more activities into less time. I've always had the notion that busyness must be related to godliness. Yet recently, in the midst of trying to get a hold of just what it means to be Christlike in today's hurried life, I am beginning to see that time management may be about doing less. There are many opportunities to minister for which I cannot plan, calls to serve that can't be scheduled in advance. Time management is life management, discerning priorities, having the right perspective, claiming responsibility for my time, accepting interruptions as opportunities, learning when to delegate and when to say no, and feeling good about the choices I have made.

Has Anyone Seen My Time?

The statement, "She has more time than I do," reflects an obvious misconception. I am reminded of games we played as children, using an hourglass timer. Without fail, someone during the game would exclaim, "It's not fair. The sand emptied faster on me. I didn't have as much time as you did!"

Guess what? God is fair. Each of us gets 24 hours a day—no more, no less. Each hour is divided into 60 minutes, 3,600 seconds. The difference comes in what we do with our 24 hours. Another person may get more use out of her 3,600 seconds each hour, but she gets not one second more. There is no way to put an extra hour here or an extra day there, but we can learn to make the best use of the time we have. When we master our time, we master our lives.

That is what Christian time management is all about. As we begin to listen for and abide by God's plan for our time, we learn to master, not be mastered, by it. The apostle Paul said it well, "Be very careful, then, how you live—not as unwise but as wise, making the most of every opportunity, because the days are evil" (Eph. 5:15-16).

Acknowledging God's Time

A good place to start thinking about time is the Bible where we find several principles about time and our use of it.

MAKE THE TIME
Look up the following verses. What does the Bible say about time?
1. Genesis 1: 3-5, 14, 15 _____

_____
2. Psalm 74: 16_____

_____
3. Philippians 4: 19 _____

_____

2

4. Matthew 25: 29 _____

_____

5. Ephesians 5: 15, 16_____

_____

6. Colossians 4: 5 _____

_____

These passages remind us God created time and it belongs to Him just as our money, talents, and children do. If we acknowledge God's ownership of time, we must also acknowledge that He can stretch it to fit our needs. God will supply all our needs (Phil. 4:19), including time. This realization, while relieving us from worry about not having enough time, also indicates that we need to distinguish time *needed* and time *desired*. God doesn't give us a greater number of minutes, but instead, helps us use the minutes more efficiently. He increases the quality of what we produce in the amount of time we have.

God's time has been given to us to use, to invest for a little while. The Lord's instruction about being a good steward applies to our use of time as well as talents, resources, and money. Paul instructed the early church to "make the best possible use of your time" (Col. 4:5 Phillips). The Ephesians were charged to use their time wisely and to "make the most of every opportunity you have for doing good" (Eph. 5:16 TLB).

We will also be asked to account for how we spent our time just as the servants in Jesus' parable: "For the man who uses well what he is given shall be given more, and he shall have abundance. But from the man who is unfaithful, even what little responsibility he has shall be taken from him" (Matt 25:29 TLB).

A Look at the Master Manager

As Christians we would be negligent if we did not look at the life of Jesus for some hint as to how to better organize our time. All four Gospel writers present a picture of Jesus under constant pressure, being pursued by friends and enemies, acquaintances and strangers. His every word was monitored, every gesture commented on, every action analyzed.

Although His world was much different from ours, it would appear that Jesus lived with intrusions and demands similar to ours. Jesus worked long, full days. Matthew writes that after one strenuous day of teaching, Jesus fell asleep on a boat. Even

3

a storm did not wake Him. Jesus quite often worked well into the night. After describing one busy day, Mark records "that evening at sundown, they brought to him all who were sick or possessed with demons."

Even so, I never get the feeling that He was rushed, that He had to play "catch up," or that He was taken by surprise. He had time for people, spending hours talking to people like Zaccheus or the Samaritan woman at the well. He spent time with friends like Lazarus, Mary, and Martha; He attended a wedding feast and other social events. His life showed a wonderful balance, a holy sense of time.

Not only was He adept at handling His public time without an appointment secretary; He managed adequate amounts of time alone for the purpose of prayer, meditation, and being with the few that gathered around Him as family and teammates. He really was the Master Manager.

In *Ordering Your Private World*, Gordon MacDonald notes three reasons why Jesus commanded control of His time. First, He understood His mission. Second, Jesus realized that time must be set aside for gathering power and inner strength. And finally, He budgeted His time, giving priority to the training of the 12 disciples. Let's look at these reasons in more detail to see how they might apply to our personal time management.

First, Jesus clearly understood His mission. With a key task to perform, He measured His use of time against that sense of mission. Even as a youth talking with the temple leaders, Jesus explained to His mother, "I must be about my Father's business" (Luke 2:49 KJV). Several other times in His short ministry Jesus was able to say, "The right time for me has not yet come," (John 7:6) or "my appointed time is near" (Matt 26:18). Because He had a clear vision of His mission, not even Satan could convince Him to shortcut His Father's eternal priorities.

Second, Jesus understood His own limitations but He also knew the source of His power. When He came to earth He set aside certain rights as the Prince of Heaven and accepted, for a time, human limitations. After launching His ministry, Jesus realized that properly budgeting His time would compensate for human weaknesses when spiritual warfare begins.

Jesus prayed daily as He awaited the Father's instructions. Before He began His public ministry, He spent 40 days in the wilderness communing with the Father. He was prepared for

Satan's temptation even before the attack. He spent the night in prayer before He chose the 12 disciples. Recall the early morning vigil on the mountainside after a busy time in Capernaum, the withdrawal to the Mount of Transfiguration to prepare for His final trek into Jerusalem and finally, Gethsemane. Such private moments were a fixed item on Jesus' time budget. He not only knew His limits; He also knew the source of His strength.

Another important element of Jesus' time management was that He made intentional choices about His time. With a world to reach, Jesus planned and budgeted His time and used His moments wisely. Jesus invested prime time taking the disciples through the Scriptures and sharing heavenly insights. He spent key moments sharing ministry with individuals, permitting them to watch every action and hear every word. Special days were set aside to explain to His disciples the deeper meaning of His messages to the crowds. Valuable hours were seized in order to debrief them when they returned from assignments, to rebuke them when they failed, and to affirm them when they succeeded. He understood the importance of the future work of these chosen few and knew their training must be a priority. He practiced the principle: where your priorities are, there your time will be.

For reasons like these, Jesus was never caught short on time. He knew His mission; He was spiritually sharpened by moments alone with God; and He used wisdom when choosing the focus of His time and energy. Remarkably, at the end of three short years of ministry, He was able to say, "I have finished the work which thou gavest me to do" (John 17:4 KJV). He accomplished the task He had been assigned.

These three time management principles evident in the life of the Master Manager provide a framework for the remaining chapters of this book. To command control of our time we must discover our own purpose as followers of Christ and must establish priorities in line with this purpose. Just as Jesus was spiritually sharpened by moments alone with God, we, too, must budget time for instruction and guidance from the Lord.

CHAPTER TWO

First Things First

But seek first his kingdom and his righteousness,
and all these things will be given to you as well (Matt. 6:33).

The Master Manager reminds us that in order to gain control of our time, we must clearly understand our mission and measure our use of time against that understanding. To budget our time more effectively, we must first establish priorities within the framework of our life's calling, then set concrete goals to help us live in keeping with those priorities.

MAKE THE TIME
1. Read Luke 18. How does Jesus illustrate the importance of focusing on priorities? _____

_____

2. What do your consider your number one mission in life?

_____

3. What are some other things that God has called you to do?

_____

4. In what way do (or should) these priorities influence your time schedule? _____

_____

Seeking First the Kingdom

One of the first steps in becoming a better life manager is, like Jesus, to have a clear sense of purpose. What are we to be about as people of God? We are to be His witnesses, to share His love with those about us. If this is my mission, how should I be spending my time?

As followers of Christ we quickly claim "Seek ye first the kingdom of God" as a directive for living. But what does this mean?

As a young Christian, I was guided by the thought, "God first, others second, myself last." Struggling with my own understanding of what that meant, I concluded that my church life, reading my Bible, and praying were my most important responsibilities, then seeking to meet the needs of others came next. My personal desires were to be tended if there was any time left. Years later I began to realize that life couldn't be divided into nice little sections labeled "spiritual," "relational," and "personal." My spiritual life was related to my relationships; my personal life impacted my spiritual life; my relationships influenced my personal life.

Seeking first the kingdom of God is a command about lordship. And *lordship* is more than God first, others second, myself last. God is concerned about and involved with all of my life. All of life is spiritual. Everything I do has religious significance. "Whatever you do," Paul tells us, "do it all in the name of the Lord Jesus" (Col. 3:17). We're not to serve Jesus first, then family, then church, and on down a list. Rather, we are to serve Jesus as we serve our family, church, work, community, and our own needs.

This realization has helped me in two ways. First, it affirms that everything I do is important to God. He is concerned about, and seeks to be a part of, every aspect of my life. Second, this truth relieves much of my guilt about not spending enough time on spiritual things. My personal devotional life and efforts to know God more intimately are vital and deserve deliberate planning, but I need not feel guilty and conclude that since only 45 minutes (only 1.5 percent) of my day is set aside for spiritual concerns, God isn't a priority. I must seek God all during the day. I must begin my day asking How can I seek the kingdom of God today? and let that question carry me all through the day. With this mind set, I give the Lord not just 45 minutes, but all 24 hours of my day.

Making Time to Seek the Kingdom

What does seeking the kingdom of God mean? Look for the second coming? Prepare for life hereafter? Try to make life on earth like heaven? Jesus' command to seek first the kingdom of God is a call to take on a new value system and a challenge to embrace a new attitude. In *The Gift of Time*, William T. McConnell gives a fresh understanding of these instructions from the Lord, McConnell concludes that seeking the kingdom is a basic attitude which defines a Christian's priorities. It is a commitment to know God, to take on His character, to serve Him, to represent Him in all aspects of our lives, and to bring others to Him. Let's look at those five aspects of our Christian commitment to seek first the kingdom of God.

1. To know God

Seeking first the kingdom of God implies the need to set aside time to get to know God, His ways, and His desires. Imagine the relationship that would result from a husband and wife who shared a general commitment but never saw or talked to one another. As seekers after God we must plan into our day, our week, and our year, times to read and study the Bible, pray, and worship, both individually and corporately.

2. To take on His character

It is only as we spend time with the Lord that we begin to take on His likeness. I am daily amazed at how much my two-year-old daughter is a miniature of myself. Though Kelsey now delights in intentionally mimicking my words and reactions, most of the responses happen naturally. They are a product of her time spent with me. If a toddler can take on the character of another in just a few short months, imagine the possibilities over a lifetime if we were only willing to spend time with the Lord. What an awesome adventure—to be like Jesus.

3. To serve Him

As we become committed to taking on Christ's character, we will naturally seek to serve Him, follow His teachings, and obey His commands—love others, seek justice, work toward harmony in our world, minister to those in need. This service would include those closest to us, our extended family, those in our Christian community, and the needy in general. Galatians 6:10 admonishes, "As we have opportunity, let us do good to all people, especially to those who belong to the family of believers." Opportunities for doing good are all around us, but how much of our time is spent taking advantage of them?

4. To represent Him in every aspect of our life

The story is told of a young boy who stood shivering in the

cold near a New York subway station. From a large, poor, single-parent home, selling newspapers was his contribution to the limited family income. As the people rushed busily in and out of the station, few seemed to notice the child, and even fewer stopped to trade their 50 cents for his papers. Suddenly an unexpected gush of wind loosened the papers from the boy's clutch, scattering them across the pavement. The boy rushed frantically to gather the pages, but it seemed that the more he rushed, the more papers he dropped. As the wind blew on, so did his means of buying his family a loaf of bread.

A businessman noticed his plight and at the risk of missing his train, stopped to gather the remains of the boy's papers. As the man smoothed the crumpled papers, he placed them in the boy's hands, along with a crisp five-dollar bill. Graciously the boy thanked him and the man hurried on his way. Soon the man was distracted by a tug on his coattail. As he turned, he looked at the tear-stained face of the young paperboy who inquired, "Hey Mister, hey Mister, are you Jesus?"

We are called to represent Christ, to be His spokesmen, to be His incarnation, to continue His work. We are to be bridge builders, connecting others to Him.

5. To bring others to Him

The logical outgrowth of building bridges that connect individuals to God's redemptive love is the growth of the kingdom. This is evangelism . . . providing an opportunity for others to experience the redemptive love of God. The imperative in The Great Commission is not "to go." Jesus knew we would always be on the go. Rather, He instructed, "*As you go*, make disciples." While you are about your daily tasks, share the good news. This is life-style evangelism. Be constantly on the lookout for opportunities to pick up someone's papers, to represent God, to bring others to Him.

MAKE THE TIME

Review the five steps for seeking the kingdom. What kind of grade would you give yourself on each of these aspects of your Christian commitment?

1. _____

2. _____

3. _____

4. _____

5. _____

Evaluating Your Use of Time

After being reminded of these steps in seeking the kingdom of God, we must stop and ask ourselves: Does the use of my time reflect these priorities? To answer this question honestly, the use of a time management tool, a time log, may be beneficial.

To make a time log, write down how you actually spend your time during the day. Every hour or so, write down what you did in the preceding time period. Because the purpose of this exercise is to get the facts out before your memory has a chance to blur them, do not wait until evening to fill in the blanks. Do this for an entire week to get a reasonably accurate picture of your actual time usage.

This exercise may prove harder than you think. You may complain that this is not a typical week or you may find yourself fitting in something spiritual just so it will appear on the charts. No week is typical; just record your activities and resist the temptation to embellish or tamper with your results.

Another way to analyze how you are spending your time is to break your days into categories. These categories might have to do with relationships, such as time spent with family, friends, co-workers, church family, and yourself. They might have to do with types of tasks, such as professional, home, volunteer, or personal time.

This exercise often helps people recognize illusions about their time usage. For example, many people believe their time is governed by external forces when in reality they allow their time to be dominated. Some people think they can use their time in any way they wish. However, just the business of living takes up all but a small part of our time. This makes it all the more important to know what we do with our time rather than lose it by default.

After looking over your time inventory, you may want to make some changes—what the Bible calls *repentance*. For some, this may mean a drastic change, such as changing jobs because you are not in a place where you can make any meaningful progress toward the goals of the kingdom. But for most of us it will mean identifying the daily opportunities which come our way. It will mean eliminating the items which contribute nothing toward the fulfillment of our Christian purpose, and instead, seeking God's guidance in shaping a more ministering life-style.

As you follow the example of the Master Manager and gain an understanding of your personal mission, you can begin to gain control of your life and your time.

Setting Goals for Your Time

Once we have acknowledged our Christian purpose, it is important to set goals—to have a plan for life and a strategy of attack. There is nothing like trying to get somewhere without directions; what a real waste of time! "In his heart a man plans his course, but the Lord determines his steps" (Prov. 16:9).

Just after Christmas one year, Rich and I were going to Mississippi to celebrate the holidays with his parents. We had only made a few trips there from seminary in Louisville but felt fairly comfortable with the anything-but-straight route we had to follow. After spending several hours on the Natchez Trace, a beautiful but desolate stretch of limited-access highway, we looked at our map. Surely there had to be a more direct route. There was no definite road marked on the map but surely if we headed in the general direction, we would reach Highway 84. We put away the map and ventured on.

You can finish the story yourself. Soon it was apparent that the path we had chosen was even worse than the original route. The roads grew smaller and undoubtedly less traveled. We maneuvered through detours, flooded and washed-out roads, retracing many of our previous paths. Soon it was obvious—we were lost. We had no idea where we were and no idea how to find out. There were no road markers, signs, businesses, or even houses. This really was the middle of nowhere! We couldn't tell which direction we were traveling and really didn't know which direction we needed to go.

We finally stopped and mapped out our game plan. We would look for larger, better maintained roads in hopes that they would lead us to a marked highway. We drove for what seemed like hours and finally began to feel that yes, this is going to work. Finally! A two-lane road (one with paint marks down the center) and then a few minutes later, a divided highway. Success! The only problem—we had no idea which direction we needed to go. We weren't even sure which state we were in.

It was early evening by now and the roadside businesses

were already closed. A glance at the sun and a guess later, we turned onto the road and were headed toward . . . somewhere. Soon we came upon a mile marker, mile marker 3 . . . Oh good! We must be three miles from something, in one direction or the other. All we had to do was ride until we found the next marker. If it was a 2, we were headed toward a major intersection. If it was a 4, we just had to turn around and go four miles in the other direction. Here it comes, the next marker. Yeah, it's a 2, and then 1, and then . . . a familiar (but unexpected) sign. Welcome to Mississippi. Welcome to Mississippi? Yes, we had driven for over an hour and were right back where we started from. Our haphazard adventure had taken us nowhere!

Often that is how it is with our daily lives. We get up in the morning, go through the motions, stay very busy, even get tired, but at the end of the day we look back and ask, *What did I accomplish?* We often accomplish so little and waste so much time because we do not know where we are going.

The Value of Goals

The first step in fulfilling our God-given purpose is to establish some directions by setting some precise goals. Goals focus on the future, allowing us to dream dreams. They help us project our present desires and dreams into future realities. When it comes to being better managers of our time, goals are essential. As seekers of the kingdom, we all need specific goals to help us in the venture and to guide us in the use of our time.

Why do goals keep us from wasting time? They motivate us to take action, help us make decisions, protect us from false urgency, allow us to measure progress, and help us control stress. Let's look at these reasons in a little more detail.

1. Goals as motivators

When you feel bored or discouraged, it is not because you have run out of things to do, but because you have run out of goals. Goals motivate us to take action. Like roadside mile markers, they allow us to see how far we have come and how far we need to go. Goals keep us from wasting time by helping us know what to do next.

2. Goals as tools for decision-making

Goals help us make decisions based not on immediate emotions but rather on sound judgment. Jesus' initial response to the word that Lazarus was critically ill must have been the desire to go immediately to His sick friend. Yet, thoughtfully, He continued in His ongoing task. Later He was able to demonstrate God's power by bringing Lazarus back to life. While His emotions surely urged Him to save a dying friend, Jesus knew that His ultimate goal was to save a dying world.

3. Goals as protection from false urgency

It has been said that the important things in life are seldom urgent, and the urgent things are seldom important. The account of Mary and Martha verifies that claim. Martha became entangled in the urgent matter of preparing a meal for the Lord while her sister, Mary, focused on the important matter of sitting with the Lord.

As many of us do, Martha became a victim of false urgency. We tell ourselves that time with God and our family is important. We believe that building relationships is important. We know that developing our spiritual lives is important, but how much time do we spend on these essentials? Often we fail to transform these beliefs into specific goals, and we become victims of the urgent rather than doers of the important.

4. Goals as tools for measuring progress

Goals keep us from wasting time by showing us how far we've come. When there is nothing by which to measure our progress toward fulfillment in life, our time will disappear as mysteriously as money in a poorly managed bank account.

5. Goals as stress reducers

We can see that stress and the achievement of goals is closely related. One suggestion for reducing time stress is to focus on the accomplishments rather than the time involved. By concentrating our efforts toward meeting certain goals, we find personal guidelines, direction, and much of the stress of just doing, doing, doing can be reduced.

A Variety of Goals

It is important to set both long- and short-range goals. Long-range goals give us a vision that beckons us on when short-range goals begin to look tedious. The vision of a finished product (for example, this manuscript in an actual book form) often compels me to sit at the computer a little longer in order to complete one more section.

Similarly, short-range goals help us to see how our long-range tasks can actually be reached. If my long-range goal is to have a meaningful one-hour quiet time by the end of the year, examples of accompanying short-range goals might be to maintain an effective prayer diary, to read several publications about establishing a quiet time, to develop a habit of daily setting aside time for Bible study. By setting and reaching manageable short-range goals, long-range goals become attainable.

Goals should include several basic characteristics.

•They should be worthwhile. Choose goals that are important to you and worth all the effort it will take to achieve them.

•Goals should be specific and measurable (for example, to lose ten pounds by next year).

•They should be attainable—not so low that they offer no challenge (to lose a pound) but not so high as to be discouraging (to look like Miss America by next week).

•Goals should be flexible. Remember, circumstances change and priorities shift. Don't be so rigid that you fail to be sensitive to the need to alter your personal goals.

•Goals should be written. List your goals; this helps you visualize your objectives, strengthen your commitment, and provide a basis for reviewing and checking your progress.

MAKE THE TIME

Goals should cover various aspects of our lives. Take time to set some goals for your life, both long-range and short-range in the following areas. Keep in mind the principles about goal setting: goals should be specific, measurable, attainable, written, scheduled, and flexible.

physical

spiritual

financial

personal

relational

educational

occupational

social

Commit these goals to prayer. Share them with a close friend or your spouse. Mull over them and return to them in several days to revise and polish them. Take note of the benefits of achieving these goals and some of the obstacles you will face in pursuing them. Think about what you need to help you realize these goals. Then, use these goals as the Master Manager did—to help provide direction and structure as you move toward organization of your life and your time.

CHAPTER THREE

Planning in the Quiet Times

Reverence for God adds hours to each day (Prov. 10:27 TLB).

The Master Manager not only knew His purpose and mission in life. By His example He taught us the importance of regularly spending time seeking direction and gathering strength to accomplish that mission. Again, Luke's account of Mary and Martha provides a vivid lesson of how we should spend our time. Like Martha, I seem to be so focused on doing good things to please God that I don't take the time for the best—to do as Mary did and sit at the Lord's feet—to hear Him, to learn from Him, and to enjoy His presence in my life.

While time management experts may suggest we be like Martha and get more done in less time, Jesus said it was Mary who chose the good thing. He never said that Martha's choice was bad. Jesus was continually instructing His disciples to follow and to do. He must have been telling us that there is a time for service in the name of our Lord, but only after we have taken the time to be fed, replenished, and restored in God's presence. When we become more deliberate sitting at Jesus' feet, the Martha-tasks more easily fall into place. It is in the daily process of taking the time to sit at the Lord's feet, periodically setting aside time to climb a mountain as Jesus did, and even in taking regular time off that we identify and gain the power to live out our priorities.

Taking Time to Sit at the Lord's Feet

At one point in my life daily devotional time I jumped from one method to another, trying to find just the right one for me, being easily distracted from the task by interruptions and other responsibilities. My quiet time had become like my piano practicing as a child. I would stall, delay, make excuses, and finally, when feeling forced or guilty, I hurriedly rushed through every piece just so I could tell my Mom that I really had practiced. The results were obvious. Little serious effort produced meager progress and a lot of guilt and frustration.

Similarly, I felt guilty when, in my busyness, my quiet time would wane into a time for planning, list making, and organizing my day. Somehow, even through the guilt, the activity seemed to have sort of a sacred effect when first thing in the morning I thought over my day and made lists, schedules, and agendas, and then prayed about the tasks of the day. I knew it wasn't what all the books said to do in a quiet time, but part of it felt right. While preparing to write this book, I read a chapter in William McConnell's *The Gift of Time* that was one of those true "ah ha" experiences. The author read my mind and was expressing my own frustration with my personal quiet time!

McConnell explains that when we read a prepared devotion or a few verses of Scripture out of context, our quiet time is isolated from the concerns of our normal daily activities. What we read or pray rarely has a direct bearing on how we use our time. He suggests that we make our devotional time more connected with our everyday life. If our personal planning and time management includes space for a quiet time, why shouldn't our quiet time contribute to our planning or time management?

McConnell suggests that if we included a time for planning in our quiet time, we could orient our entire day toward God instead of trying to find a few moments here and there to squeeze Him in. By including planning as a part of our quiet time, four things happen: our devotions are not separated from the rest of our activities; our planning can be done in the context of prayer and God's Word; we affirm constantly our commitment to the purpose and values of the kingdom of God; we experience the guidance of the Holy Spirit in establishing our priorities and plans.

The Reformer's Method

Godly time planning is not really a new method at all. Martin Luther described his own devotional habits in a letter published in 1535 with the title "A Simple Way to Pray, for a Good

Friend." Walter Trobisch, in a booklet titled *Martin Luther's Quiet Time* applies Luther's method of conducting a quiet time to modern-day time planning.

Luther included the elements of devotion that we normally associate with a quiet time—Bible study and prayer. He suggests that we read a short passage and not take too much upon ourselves lest the spirit get tired.

"It is sufficient to grasp one part of a Bible verse or even half a part from which you can strike a spark in your heart . . . for the soul, if it is directed towards one single thing . . . if it is really serious about it, can think more in one moment than the tongue can speak in ten hours and the pen can write in ten days," said Luther.

Trobisch reiterates that it is more fruitful to take a short passage and "shake each verse like the branches of a tree until some fruit falls down" than to struggle with a lengthy segment of Scripture.

Four Essential Questions

After choosing a Scripture passage (using a devotional book, missions periodical, or prayer guide) read it several times. Luther suggested that we begin reflecting on the chosen words by asking several questions. This process helps to create the right frame of mind. The exercise stimulates active study—looking for something, not just letting the ideas flow by.

The first questions one should ask focus attention on our relationship with God, through thanksgiving and confession. First ask, *What am I grateful for? What in the text leads me to thanksgiving?* Then ask, *What do I regret? What makes me sad? What do I need to confess concerning this text?*

The second set of questions deals with our response to God in our daily life through intercession and obedience. Ask, *How should this passage impact how I pray? Does the text lead me to intercede, either for myself or for others?* And finally, *What am I to do? What does the Lord require of me here?*

Because our thoughts can not stay on the text we are studying, even distractions can be part of our devotion. Luther concluded that when your "thoughts go for a walk" give room to these thoughts, listen to them in silence and not suppress them. "Here the Holy Spirit Himself is preaching and one word of His sermon is better than thousands of our own prayers." We will often want to thank God for people and events, confess sins, and voice concerns that have little or nothing to do with the passage chosen. With each question ask, *What other things can I thank God for, confess, or pray about?*

Moving Toward Daily Planning

The fourth question, *What should I do?* links our quiet time to how we plan the use of the rest of our time. McConnell concludes that this is the revolutionary aspect of Luther's devotional plan. No longer can our quiet time be a strictly spiritual exercise. Instead, it becomes a family council with the Father, a huddle with the Coach, a board meeting with the Boss.

Using this process, our daily to-do list will come out of our time with God. The text we are reading may point out specific things to be done. (For example: do not let the sun go down on your wrath; honor your father and your mother; do not speak evil against one another; love your neighbor.) Other times the Spirit may bring to mind someone or some task which normally we would not have thought of. Just as Ananias was instructed to visit Saul (Acts 9:10-19), we may be led to include in our plans things we might have otherwise known nothing about or certainly avoided if we had known.

Although this kind of guidance seems somewhat mystical we must be reminded of how different God's ideas of managing the kingdom are from ours. Beware though—the devil can disguise his voice to sound like the Holy Spirit, and the Christian can be easily misled. Many times we confuse our own interests with what we think God wants us to do. Just as God did not normally speak to Ananias directly as recorded in Acts, we should not expect direct guidance to be God's standard. Yet, there are too many witnesses to God's occasional direct guidance for us to reject it. With time we learn to better discern the Spirit's voice from our own thoughts.

Besides bringing to mind the things that we should do, planning in our devotional life often reveals things that we are not suppose to do. Peter Drucker, author of *The Effective Executive*, calls these tasks *posteriorities*—those things which must be avoided or eliminated if we are to accomplish our priorities. A great sense of freedom can result from discovering that something we thought was necessary really doesn't have to be done.

Of course, most of our time is concerned with normal day-today responsibilities: our families, work, church, civic duties, and so on. Thoughts about these "things to do" often intrude into our quiet time. Instead of trying to dismiss these thoughts as secular concerns, sent from the devil to disrupt your spiritual devotion, McConnell suggests that we take time to write them down. This serves to both free our mind of them and also to help us determine our priorities or identify our posteriorities. In praying about each of these responsibilities, we can get a clearer idea of how each contributes to the kingdom of God.

A quiet time need not be totally private; sharing with someone is an important part of any devotional life. But especially in this quiet time where decisions are made and one's time is planned, it is essential to share with others who must coordinate their activities with ours. A husband and wife who utilize the same plan will find a real sense of team work, unity, and companionship as they experience God's leadership in their individual lives as well as their marriage partnership.

A Time for Evaluation

When these four questions become a part of our devotional life, each day becomes linked to other days. Ask yourself, Did I do what was on yesterday's to-do list? Yes? Then give thanks! No? Then make that a part of your confession. What from yesterday's list needs to become part of today's list?

Asking these questions also provides an opportunity to evaluate our use of time. Why didn't I do what was on my list for yesterday? You may discover you simply had too much to do, or you underestimated how much time a certain activity would take. You may have added activities others could have done, things you thought others expected of you, or things you included hoping God would approve. Your quiet time may also show you that you need to say no more often.

Using this system, what happened yesterday becomes a matter for our next "family council" with God. Such daily huddles with the Father give us the short-term direction we need for daily living. We review past performance, check our direction, and get new marching orders for the day.

Trobisch reminds us that this kind of "warm-up training" takes practice. If we continue to practice warming up our hearts to God we will learn to walk more confidently in His guidance. This kind of quiet time is a concrete way to "seek first the kingdom of God" and see "all these things" put into proper perspective (Matt. 6:33-34). As we gain power and direction, we too can follow Christ's example and be about our Father's business.

MAKE THE TIME

1. If you are not already committed to a daily devotional time, what steps do you need to take to make this a priority?

_____

_____

2. How can you incorporate your daily planning into your time at the Lord's feet?

_____

_____

Taking Time to Climb a Mountain

On several occasions, Jesus withdrew from the crowd, taking a retreat from the busyness of life. Matthew records, "After he had dismissed them, he went up on a mountainside by himself to pray. When evening came, he was there alone" (Matt. 14:23). Similarly, Luke recounts, "But Jesus often withdrew to lonely places and prayed" (Luke 5:16). Scripture depicts Jesus retreating after busy, people-filled occasions. He knew the value of time alone to regroup, rethink, reevaluate, and refuel. It is also interesting to note that the times after this solitude were always filled with power and the miraculous—Jesus walked on water, calmed the storm, healed a paralytic.

We, too, need time in the mountains. Group worship, private devotional time, and regular Bible study are essential, but sometimes larger chunks of time are necessary to keep from getting bogged down in the details of daily living. A personal retreat gives time to look at the whole picture of one's life and to seek direction from God. Arrange a half-day retreat at the beginning of each month. You may find it difficult to set aside that large of a chunk of time, but make the extra effort to do so. The busier you are, the more you need this time. An evening, a Saturday morning, a Sunday afternoon, whenever you can—schedule it. If you cannot set aside the time monthly, consider retreating every other month or quarterly.

Write the date on your calendar and when the time comes, gather your Bible, hymnal, calendar, notebook, and pen—and leave home. One busy woman insists that leaving home is a must: "I don't want the distraction of a ringing telephone or doorbell or the sight of a cobweb to lure me away from my intended retreat."

If the weather is nice, take a blanket and sit at a nearby park. Go to the public library, a room at church, or if all else fails, sit in your parked car. Spend time reading your Bible, reading or singing hymns, evaluating progress on last month's goals, and setting new ones for the coming month. Find a specific Scripture that you can claim as a promise for the next month. You also might select a hymn. Singing or reading it for a whole month commits it to memory for you to retrieve when needed.

A monthly personal retreat can be a time for planning the coming month in as much detail as possible—noting personal, children's, spouse's, and family's commitments that concern you. Take stock of wardrobe needs, meal planning, household and cleaning projects. Try to nail down specific dates whenever possible. Sometimes you will have to change plans but you will find that knowing you have goals and plans, and knowing that you and God made them together, will give you a feeling of control over the next month. If you are married, share goals, plans, and schedules with your spouse.

Take the time to prayerfully plan, even when you feel too busy to do so. While the logical temptation is to get more time by cutting out God's share, you will find that the more the day needs stretching, the more time you must spend with God. Martin Luther said, "I have so much to do [today] that I shall spend the first three hours in prayer." I am learning from the example of Jesus that when I spend time with God it enables me to gain greater control over my time and see more clearly what God wants me to do. Ruth Miller, author of *The Time Minder*, expresses what so many have discovered when they regularly take time to climb a mountain:

> As I gave Him a few moments, He taught me how to handle the hours and the days. . . . And the more time I committed to Him, the more He expanded the time to fill my need for it. It has turned into one grand and glorious cycle of my giving my days to God and His stretching them and giving them back with just enough room . . .

Taking Time Off

The word *leisure* comes from the Latin, *licere*, meaning "to be permitted." We need to give ourselves permission to relax. We would do well to imitate our Lord's example. Following the sixth day of creation, God deliberately stopped working. He took time to relax. No, He wasn't tired. I'm sure He didn't need to recuperate. God set aside time to enjoy His creation.

Jesus recognized the importance of rest and relaxation. He frequently escaped the press of the crowd by climbing into a boat with His disciples to fish, visit, or just take a nap. He enjoyed visiting with dear friends, such as Mary, Martha, and Lazarus; He took time out to share meals and special occasions with those He loved. Read Mark 6:31.

Even with biblical examples to verify the importance of leisure, we still often feel guilty when we take the time to relax. This negative emotion is unnecessary. We need to learn to think of leisure time as something we do for God's purpose. Instead of thinking that we work in order to have leisure, it is more appropriate to realize that we spend time in leisure in order to get on with our work. Any stay-at-home Mom knows that she owes her family some time away from the job. Modern industry has learned the value of time away from work, thus coffee breaks and mandatory vacations.

We must assume responsibility for our leisure time, for rarely will someone else insist that we take it. Unfortunately, many find that planning for leisure is often more difficult than planning work. If I wait until all my work is done before I sit down to sew (one of my leisurely treats), I grow more and more frustrated because the list never gets completed and I never make it to the sewing machine. But when I schedule in an hour, say twice a week, to work on a craft project, or treat myself to 30 minutes of sewing after several hours at the computer, I feel refreshed and rewarded.

Leisure means different things to different people. My husband enjoys mowing the yard. For me, that is forced labor. My friend Sharon will sit for hours, relaxing with a good book. For me that is *bor-ing*! Leisure for some means going to the movie, entertaining guests, baking bread, going for a walk. Give me half an hour for a refreshing bicycle ride or a dip in the pool!

Sometimes it is best to take leisure as it comes, packaged in various sizes and shapes. It may come in tiny presents like a quiet bubble bath after the children are finally in bed. It may be in the form of a weekly gift—a date with our spouse or an occasional weekend retreat or get-away with a friend. Leisure, like gifts, sometimes comes in surprise packages to be ripped into and enjoyed impulsively.

One morning after Logan had gone to kindergarten, I set about on my regular straighten-up-around-the-house routine. Because Rich was gone for an out-of-town meeting, I was anxious about not being able to have my regular morning writing time. Maybe I could pull out some old packed-away toys to keep not-yet-two-year-old Kelsey entertained for a little while so I could work at the computer. I found a box of wooden spools and large pipe cleaners, and showed her how to thread them to make pretty bracelets. Taking pride in my ingenuity, I sat down in an effort to fulfill that ever-approaching manuscript deadline.

Wrong! After repeated efforts at distracting little hands from the keyboard, it soon became obvious that Kelsey was determined to make havoc out of my game plan. As an alternate plan, I decided that we could go to the grocery store to buy a few things. That would entertain her and I could still take care of one of those items on my list. Upon entering the garage, the determined shriek, "troller ride, troller ride" altered my plans another time. (Unfortunately, her scream has a way of doing that.) Oh well, getting a little exercise is always an item on the list, so I agreed, "OK, let's walk to the store."

It was a beautiful spring morning. The sun sparkling through the dew of the new green grass and the freshly plowed fields that dotted the hillsides almost instantaneously signaled to me that this was a gift. Stop and tear into it. As we strolled, we listened to "the birdies" and watched them hop across the grass. We stopped to see the just-ripening berries in a neighbor's strawberry patch and to talk to Chip (a horse) in the field down the road. Needless to say, the original ten-minute run to the neighborhood grocery stretched into a morning project. On the way home, we went on a scavenger hunt and successfully found the rooster we had heard crowing; we played "kick the can" up the sidewalk and "tight-rope" walked on a roadside retaining wall. We picked wild flowers and collected pretty rocks. And then, when we finally returned home, an hour-and-a-half later, we stopped on the porch to blow and chase bubbles.

The morning was gone, but it had not slipped into oblivion

like a thousand others, but rather into a little niche in my memory. The warmth of the sun, the joyful giggles, the simplicity and innocence of my growing-too-fast two-year-old, the wonder in those big brown eyes, and the contentment of those unhurried moments will long be remembered.

On that morning walk I spent invaluable time strengthening a relationship. And I learned a lesson as well. Taking time off for leisure does not mean taking time off from God's plan for our life. Rather, it is refreshing ourselves for the work He has for us to do. We must learn to follow the example of the Master Manager who regularly took time to pray, to plan, and even to relax. It is in taking the time for a daily quiet time, periodic getaways for planning and renewal, and regular time-off for leisure and relaxation, that we find the needed direction and strength for the journey ahead.

MAKE THE TIME
1. List some activities that you like to do to relax.
_____
_____

2. When was the last time you took time off for leisure?
_____
_____

3. How can you be more deliberate about planning for leisure? What can you do to assure that you follow through with these plans? _____
_____

CHAPTER FOUR

Seize Control of Your Time

For the man who uses well what he is given shall be given more, and he shall have abundance (Matt. 25:29 TLB).

Are you continually doing something for someone else . . . taking children to the next practice, running an errand for your spouse, stopping by the church to help with a mail-out, carrying an elderly neighbor to the doctor? Do you ever feel that everyone else has decided how you should spend your time, and you do not have any say-so? Often that seems to be the dilemma, but think again. All of these time-consuming activities are the result of a choice—your choice. You did not have to say yes. You made a conscious decision somewhere in the process. In order to be better stewards of our time, we must follow the example of Jesus, the Master Manager. We can bring our time under control as we make intentional choices about our use of time and then claim responsibility for the choices we make.

Choosing How to Spend My Time

I have finally accepted the truth that the Lord will hold me accountable for my use of time just as the servants were responsible for their investment of the master's talents. I will be asked to account for my use of my time, and I want to make sure that I'm the one who decides how I spend it. Too many others have too many ideas about how I should spend my time. If I have not thought it through and planned the use of my time, then by my own default, someone else will decide for me. Yes, I do have obligations that take up my time. But these obligations are of my choosing, not someone else's.

Let me use a personal example. We are constantly asked to make decisions about the use of our time, meeting the demands of society to be a good spouse, parent, community leader, and humanitarian. Because I have chosen marriage and a family I can accept that keeping the house clean is part of my responsibility. However, I do have choices. I can negotiate tasks with my husband and other family members, hire a maid, be satisfied with a lower standard of housekeeping, or spend most of my time doing housework.

If you feel that you are spending all your time as a chauffeur service, transporting your children from one practice to another lesson to another rehearsal, evaluate the situation. If it is important to you that your children be this involved, then accept that this time-crunch is a conscious decision you have made, and make the most of it. If, on the other hand, you feel taken advantage of or resentful, you may need to make a change. Consider limiting extra-curricular activities to a reasonable number, seeking out a carpooling plan with others, or enlisting the help of a spouse or another family member. It is important that children realize you have personal interests and obligations that are important to you, too. I have found that even after limiting two children to two outside activities, the problem is still not alleviated. Church programs, doctor and dentist appointments, not to mention parent meetings, booster clubs, and your own obligations can still leave you feeling overwhelmed by the constant rush of getting family members from activity to activity. I have to continually remind myself that I have chosen to let my children be involved in these activities; I have chosen to be an involved parent; and I am committed to my personal participation in my own activities and ministries. These obligations and responsibilities didn't just happen. When I accept these choices, I can also accept the consequences—not much "just hangin' around" time, more "quick-fix" and fast-food meals, and lower standards for a clean house. But it is not until I accept these decisions and claim responsibility for these choices that I can begin to feel in control of my time.

Time management skills are not the first step to putting order in our lives. First we must recognize that time is a gift from God, and that His priorities can always be fulfilled in the amount of time we have been given. Christ knew what He was called to do and because He made conscious decisions about when to say yes and when to say no He was able to do all that He was called to do. With this perspective one can find great freedom, a release from the expectations of society. To do God's will does not mean meeting every request that school, church, or civic groups proposes. Instead, it means knowing what God has and has not called us to do.

Making Sound Investments of Time

The servants in Jesus' parable were expected to do more than spend or consume the money entrusted to them. The landowner expected his workers to invest their portion. Similarly, we must learn how to invest our time to receive the greatest possible return for the minutes and hours God has given us. Making sound investments of our time calls for disciplined choices. In *Managing Your Life and Your Time*, Jo Berry identifies three choices we make when allocating our time: we find time, take time, and make time.

It's easy for us to apply the find-the-time technique. When we decide to do something that is outside our regular routine, we plug the activity into an empty slot. For example, you are asked to serve on a committee at church. It meets on the second Tuesday night of each month. Your Tuesday evenings are free, so you accept. You fill the time slot that is empty.

With the find-the-time technique, you simply use whatever time is available to do whatever comes along. Time, not goals or priorities, becomes the deciding factor in what you do. You agree to serve on the committee because it meets on Tuesday nights when you are not busy, not because you feel you have something to contribute, or have a burden, or are convinced that it is God's will for your life. A convenient but not very effective time investment method!

Another poor investment of one's time is the take-the-time approach. This technique requires borrowing time from one task and giving it to another task. In my case, it is usually my children or my husband who get cheated the most. People who allocate time this way are already overextended and become masters at juggling activities within their crammed schedule. Time-takers never ask themselves if they should do something; they just say yes to everything. They rarely accomplish long-range goals because they are doing too much.

You have heard it said, "you make time for the things that are important to you." The third choice we can make about our use of time is called the make-the-time technique. This method gives the best return on its investment. Time-makers are not time-finders, mindlessly filling time slots. Neither are they time-takers, juggling commitments and schedules because of over-commitment. Rather, time-makers make time by carefully planning and thoughtfully deciding how to spend unused time. They weigh their opportunities, plan how to get the best possible returns on their investment of time, and make choices based on this thoughtful preparation.

Choosing to Change

You can make time changes just as you make diet changes. Do you feel that there is too much work in your life and not enough family time? Stop working overtime and schedule a few family outings. Too much housekeeping and not enough time for personal pursuits? Let the dust accumulate for a few days. Too much tennis and not enough time for ministry to others? It doesn't take a time management expert to see what you need to do. It is a matter of deciding and following through.

Once you have made prayerful decisions about your time, accept with confidence the choices you have made and begin to take control of your time. In doing so, know that in time, your goals will change and so must your choices about time. Take the time to evaluate those choices periodically. Also realize that your choices will not necessarily be the same as someone else's. You have chosen what you feel is right for you in your present circumstances. There is no need to feel guilty because others have chosen differently. At the same time, be willing to accept the decisions that others have made about their time.

Because you are the master of your time and must answer to God for its wise use, it is up to you to take responsibility for the choices you make. You must continually sort through the opportunities available to you and sift out those which do not fit into the life-plan God has shown you. And, when faced with an overwhelming number of obligations and a limited amount of time, stop and ask yourself, Is time the problem, or am I the problem? Then do something about it. Managing your time is important, but you will never do this until you learn to manage yourself. As we learn to get control of our time and our life, we discover, ironically, greater freedom in the use of our time.

MAKE THE TIME
Take a few minutes to reflect on these questions.
1. In what areas of your life do you feel out of control?

_____

_____

2. In what areas do your responsibilities and time demands seem to snowball? _____

_____

3. What are some of the choices you have made in the last five years that have called for deliberate decisions about your use of time? Think about some of these choices—to get married, have children, to work outside the home, to assume a new ministry position at church, to build a new home.

_____

_____

4. What choices have you made recently that have effected your time demands?

_____

_____

5. Do you need to claim responsibility for these choices so that you can better control your use of time?

_____

_____

6. Are you more of a time-taker, time-finder, or a time-maker? What can you do to be more deliberate about being a time-maker? _____

_____

CHAPTER FIVE

Walk Wisely

*Be very careful, then, how you live—not as unwise,
but as wise, making the most of every opportunity,
because the days are evil (Eph. 5:15-16).*

Live wisely . . . making the most of every opportunity! Just as Paul admonished the Colossians, we too must live wisely in order to make the most of every opportunity. Jesus did, and accomplished all that God intended for Him to do. Wisely managing our time takes planning, for planning is like a treasure map, the means of getting to your goals. Planning in order to avoid the dangers of unseized time calls for budgeting, prioritizing, and scheduling.

The Danger of Unseized Time

Using the concept of *unseized time*, Christian leader Gordon MacDonald writes, in *Ordering Your Private World*, about the danger of not being in control of our time. Unseized time is the minutes and hours in our day for which we have not planned. When we haven't thought through our day and scheduled our time, these minutes often get seized by other-than-the best demands. The author suggests several laws of unseized time, explaining what is likely to happen when we aren't in control of our time.

1. Unseized time flows toward weak areas. We often invest excessive amounts of time doing things we are not good at while the tasks we are able to do with excellence and effectiveness are preempted.

2. Unseized time is influenced by dominant people in our world.

When we do not set up our own time budgets, we find that others enter our world and force unwanted tasks on us. Due to disorganization we and those we care about the most are often deprived of our best time. Powerful people in our world will ultimately control our lives better than we do because we have not taken the initiative to command our time.

3. Unseized time surrenders to the demands of all emergencies. Those of us with responsibility for leadership find ourselves continually surrounded by events that cry out for immediate attention. As Christian leaders we must learn that not everything that cries the loudest is the most urgent.

4. Unseized time focuses on things that gain public recognition. In other words, we are likely to give our unclaimed time to events that will bring the most immediate and greatest praise. Instead, we should focus on what is most important and claim our time before everyone and everything else does.

Budgeting Our Time

The central principle for claiming unseized time is this: time must be budgeted. Most of us learned this about money years ago. When money is limited, we must budget; when time is in limited supply, the same principle holds true. If you are concerned about organizing your time you must have a budgeting perspective. That means planning—determining ahead of time how your time is going to be allotted.

Take the Time to Plan

Often I find myself just too busy to plan! Or at least I am too busy to plan *and* do everything else I would like to get done. But I have learned that when I don't plan I frequently feel overwhelmed and am often counterproductive—wandering aimlessly about the house, shuffling clutter on my counter, or flipping through files and piles at my desk. And, just as the experts say, when I take the time to plan, I have more time. When I stop to think about what needs to be done and my priorities for the day, I approach the day in a more orderly manner.

Planning can actually improve the quality of life, giving a sense of direction and a feeling of accomplishment. It develops self-confidence, confirming and strengthening priorities.

Surprisingly, planning helps us be more flexible. It frees more time for personal choices and clears the mind of worry about what has to be accomplished. Planning is usually done first thing in the morning or at the end of the day. There are advantages to planning in the morning when you are fresh. Having just thought about what you have to do, you gain momentum and move easily into the tasks. With the day's priorities clearly in mind you are less likely to be sidetracked as you go along. Some prefer planning in the evening. Reflecting on what they have done that day helps them select what needs to be done tomorrow. Also, by having the day all set when they arise the next morning, evening planners do not waste time debating what to do. Another advantage is that their subconscious can work overnight so that when morning comes evening planners are primed and ready for action.

Besides daily planning, take time at the end of the week to review the week's progress and make general plans for the week to come. This is when you may need to take the time to share and compare plans, schedules, and commitments with spouse, family members, or co-workers. My husband and I use Sunday afternoon as planning time. We both spend some time alone, reviewing accomplishments, listing upcoming responsibilities, filling in our calendars, and then we get together to compare calendars, discuss car pool and child-care responsibilities for our children, and negotiate family time.

In all planning, whether long-, middle-, or short-range, you must complete two tasks: (1) make a list, and (2) set priorities, deciding what is most important to you right now.

Keep a To-do List

Most everyone practices the exercise of making a to-do list when life gets particularly hectic and the schedule gets tight. But the key to finding extra time daily is to make a to-do list every single day. Edward Dayton in *Tools for Time Management* suggests that making such a list accomplishes several things. First, you realize what lies ahead and can therefore set priorities. Second, you are able to visualize the tasks ahead of you. Third, you are able to cluster related tasks. It relieves you of the worry that accompanies trying to remember what you need to do. And finally, you have a sense of accomplishment when you cross items off the list.

The principle of keeping a to-do list is simple: on a piece of paper list the tasks that need to be accomplished that day; cross them off as they are completed and add others as they occur to you; rewrite the list at the end of the day or when it becomes difficult to read.

There are two hints to remember. First, write your list. Don't try to keep your to-do list in your head. It just isn't as effective. It is like going to the grocery store without a written shopping list. You spend a good deal of time wandering the aisles waiting for that forgotten item to jump out at you. Why clutter your mind with things that can be written down? Leave your mind free for more creative pursuits.

Second, write all of your to-do items on a master list rather than jotting them down on various scraps or notepads that you are always shuffling to find. Prepared to-do lists can be purchased or you might want to consider writing the list in your appointment book or in a notebook.

What belongs on the list? Some people list everything they have to do including routine items. Others write down only the extraordinary tasks. Others include categories, such as: what I will do and what I might do, or what has to be done and what I'd like to do. I suggest that you list everything that has a high priority or that might not get done without special attention.

Prioritize Your List—As Easy as ABC

Once the list is made, look it over. What can be delegated? What items can be left undone? What tasks are most important? Some begin at the top of the list and work down with little regard for importance. I like to pick out the easiest tasks. They're usually quicker to complete and I love to mark items off my list. But the problem is that I have a strong tendency to get bogged down with those least important items. Sometimes I say that I am getting the little things out of the way so that I will be free to tackle the big tasks. In actuality, I never get around to the big jobs because I keep finding little chores and activities to take care of, leaving important tasks unaccomplished.

The most effective way to tackle a to-do list is to prioritize. After listing the tasks that you feel need to be accomplished, categorize them according to importance. Dru Scott, in *How to Put More Time in Your Life*, suggests picturing time demands as a target. The outer circle is reserved for small tasks that consume your day, the middle circle contains secondary matters (worthwhile demands but not the best thing to do right now). The center of the target holds central concerns and essentials (time investments that contribute directly to what you want most out of life). When trying to decide what you need to do, shoot for the bull's-eye.

The most popular method for prioritizing is the ABC system. Put an *A* (absolutely must get done) by those items on your list that have high value; a *B* (better get done) by those having medium value, and a *C* (could do or could let slide) by those with lowest value. This is all sort of a guessing game and quite relative. The *A*'s change depending on what is on your list. They usually stand out clearly in contrast to the *B*s. Your ABCs may change over time. Today's *A*'s may become tomorrow's *C*s and yesterday's *B* may become today's *A*. You must continually re-evaluate your priorities, considering the best use of your time right now. After ranking your to-do list with ABCs, you may need to further break down an item to 123s, identifying specific tasks that must be completed in order to accomplish your goal.

Tackling the Tasks

Some days you may get all the *A*s and *B*s on your list done; other days you won't even finish the *A*'s. You will find that often, if you delay response, many of the *C*s can be dropped from your list completely. One rarely reaches the end of a to-do list. It is not completing the list that counts but making the best use of your time. Review the list at the end of the day or the beginning of the next. Add what needs to be added from the old to the new to-do list, and omit those items that can be left undone. Some of yesterday's *B*s may have become today's *A*'s but also some became today's *C*s or can be omitted entirely. Prioritize the new list and begin again, finding satisfaction in completing those priority tasks.

When we finally decide what is important and what tasks need to be accomplished today, we are often still reluctant to get started. Overwhelmed by an *A* task, we often turn to a few short and easy *C*s, suggesting to ourselves that we need a larger block of time before we get started. The problem is, those large blocks of uninterrupted time seldom arise. So go on and start on an *A* task even if you have to spread the task over several small blocks of time.

First, fill in those activities for which you have already made time commitments, such as meetings and appointments. Next, take your prioritized to-do list and start assigning tasks in the open slots. Group similar items together, such as errands, phone calls, or correspondence. Focus your energies on the tasks that have the greatest value. Schedule the *A* tasks first, then move on to *B* items, and then to the *C* tasks if there is still time. Be realistic when you begin to schedule your list. Allow plenty of time to accomplish each task. Be sure to build in "slack time"—a quarter to a third of your day—for unplanned demands on your time. Allow even more than that if you have small children. Don't try to schedule yourself too optimistically or you'll find yourself frustrated.

Keep a Weekly Schedule

In laying out a weekly schedule the key is to block out time for those big tasks, tough jobs, or goal-oriented projects. Reserve particular days of the week, such as Tuesday and Thursday mornings, for major projects. Or set aside time every day for the important tasks and refuse to get distracted by the less important items. Start small by allocating 15 minutes a day to use exclusively for important items.

Try blocking *A* time (for those *A* items) horizontally on a weekly calendar—at the same time each day, Monday through Friday. I am slowly learning the importance of blocking out time for those *A* tasks. While preparing this manuscript I found that I had to set aside time specifically to write. Honestly, there were too many other projects that I wanted to do more or felt like had to be done. I found that it was just too easy to find other activities to do. At the end of each day I would say, *Gee I just didn't have much time to write today.* But I knew this was a commitment I had made and a goal I wanted to accomplish, so in order to complete the task I had to block out time.

First, I started with a block of time in the morning from 9 until 11, three days a week. It took awhile for me to give this time priority treatment, but I finally learned to say to myself, *I can take care of that chore this afternoon*; and to say to others, *No, but I can meet after 11.* When my husband began to see that I was serious about blocking out the time, he took greater care in helping me protect that time. Soon, I was able to add two other days to the writing schedule. I was finally learning that old planning principle: there is always enough time for those things that are important to you.

Personalize Your Scheduling System

Keeping a good time–scheduling system will do four things:
1. provide balance between short– and long–range planning.
2. provide a record of what has been done as well as what needs to be done.
3. be accessible to others (family, spouse, work associates) who have reason to know what your future commitments are.
4. be a simple, habit-forming system that does not take too much time to prepare, maintain, or use.

There are numerous systems for scheduling—pocket calendars, personal organizers, desk or wall calendars. Calendars may be organized by months, weeks, and days. Some appointment books have hour-by-hour scheduling. Some choose to use a notebook with calendar entries as well as pages for keeping goals and lists. Many personal computers have programs for designing your own calendar. Construct your personal plan of scheduling and planning and make it a daily habit.

Priority Calendaring

I have been slow to learn the truth that the non-essential items crowd into the date book long before the necessities. An interesting truth is that those most important time allocations never seem to scream out immediately when ignored. When we neglect our spiritual disciplines here and there, God does not shout loudly about it. We can make it fine for awhile. And when we do not allocate time for our family, they generally are understanding and forgiving. These things can be ignored for a while without adverse effects because they often don't demand instant response and attention as do many individuals and other commitments. And that is why they are so often crowded out when we don't budget them in advance. Other, less important, issues have a way of wedging them aside week after week. Tragically, if they are neglected too long . . . when family, rest, and spiritual disciplines are finally noticed . . . it is often too late to avoid adverse consequences.

You will find a great deal of time by carefully planning whatever you really want to do. Just as the Master Manager, the busiest people are able to find the time to do what they want to do, not because they have any more time than others, but because they think in terms of "making" time by carefully planning, prioritizing, and scheduling.

MAKE THE TIME
1. Review the dangers of unsiezed time. To which ones are you most likely to fall prey?

_____

_____

2. Practice planning and prioritizing. Make a list of ten things you must do today. Prioritize your list using the ABC system. Now, try inserting these tasks into an actual schedule.

_____

_____

3. How can you improve your personal planning system?

_____

_____

CHAPTER SIX

Battling Overcommitment

You are worried and upset about many things,
but only one thing is needed (Luke 10:41-42).

I often feel that my life is like the cuddly honey-loving bear (and great philosopher) Winnie the Pooh, who frequently found himself in a bind and "wedged in with great tightness." Every part of my day is sandwiched in, yet I continue trying to make room for a little bit more. I have found that overcommitment is another major time waster. Recall Jesus' words to Martha: "You are worried and upset about many things, but only one thing is needed" (Luke 10:41-42). Jesus reminded us of the danger of trying to do too much. He personally made use of tools for battling overcommitment, including separating the urgent from the important, saying no, and delegating.

Separating the Urgent from the Important

As Christians we live in constant tension between the urgent and the important. We are often tempted to let urgent tasks crowd out the most important. They call for instant action— endless demands that seem to pressure every hour of every day. We can all recall Christmases where we spent so much energy in preparation that when the great and holy day finally arrived we were too exhausted to enjoy it. Or what school-teacher hasn't experienced days when she was so involved in the detailed demands and procedures of the day that the needs of individual children went unnoticed. I have a tendency to get so involved in providing for my children (decorating their rooms, sewing clothes, organizing shelves) that I forget that it is more important to take the time just to be with them.

The problem is that the important tasks (prayertime, quality time with my children, a date with my husband, a conversation with that non-Christian friend) rarely call out as loudly as the urgent. Because they can more easily be neglected, we often do not notice the results until it is too late.

The Master Manager's Solution

Jesus was able to tell the difference between the urgent and the important. When He was told He must go to Bethany because Lazarus was dying, He knew it was more important to continue His present task and go later to raise Lazarus from the dead. He prayerfully waited for the Father's instructions and the accompanying strength to follow them. He had no divinely-drawn blueprint; He discerned the Father's will day by day in a life of prayer, thus warding off the urgent and accomplishing the important. This gave Him a sense of direction, set a steady pace, and enabled Him to do every task the Lord had assigned so that on the last night He could say, "I have finished the work Thou gavest me to do."

How can we decide in our own lives what is important and what is urgent? Seek God's guidance as Jesus did. Pray for the Lord's direction and wait for His instructions. Reflect on your priorities. Ask yourself, *How does this request fit with my God-given priorities and goals?* Ask your family what they need. (You may see that they don't need as much from you as you thought.) Get an overview picture of how you spend your time by making a personal time inventory (see chapter two).

Another helpful tool for discerning what is really important is to ask yourself, *Will it matter five years from now?* Logan entered the kitchen and asked if I would play baseball with him. My in-laws were expected at any time and I still had a million things to do to get ready. I was torn between going out for mother/son time or staying inside in an attempt to make a good impression. I knew that in five years no one (not even my in-laws) would remember that there was dust on the piano. I went on out to "shag a few flies."

When faced with a decision about how to spend our time, we must use Christ as our example and separate the important from the urgent. If we don't, we most often will be urged to put the urgent first and give the important second place.

Saying No

Many lament the fact that they never seem to have enough time. They suffer from a common problem—a fearfulness about saying the word *no*. Why is it that one of the first words we learn to say as a child is the hardest word for many of us to say as an adult? When it comes to managing our time, *no* can be the greatest timesaving tool in the English language.

We may say yes for some wrong reasons, such as a desire to gain the approval and acceptance of others; a fear of offending friends and acquaintances; a guilty feeling of not measuring up to someone else's standards. Busyness makes some people feel important; others link overcommitment with spirituality. We are tempted to say yes because of low self-esteem and a compelling need to be needed by others or because of a tendency to overrate our own sense of importance.

Saying Yes When You Should Say No

The can't-say-no syndrome has several dangers. It leads to overcommitment which in turn contributes to stress, burnout, and poor health. The inability to say no distracts from our basic objectives. Saying yes to unending requests inevitably results in being spread so thin that the basic purposes of our calling can't be fulfilled. Family relations, friendships, jobs, and ministries are often threatened.

Not being able to say no often leaves us miserable. Do you find yourself saying, Why did I say I would do that? When we take on projects for the wrong reasons, our joy often turns to resentment. Also, saying yes when we don't have time (or don't really plan) to follow through is not fair to the other person(s) involved. Keep in mind that by saying yes when we should say no, taking on projects that God has not intended for us, we may be robbing someone else of a blessing.

Before You Say Yes

Unfortunately, people know "yessers" and take full advantage of them. The greater number of talents one possesses, the more essential is the ability to say no. In *Managing Your Life and Your Time*, Jo Berry gives guidelines to follow before you say yes.

• Break the yes habit. We often say yes out of habit, because we

41

have been conditioned to do so. Saying yes is easier and more comfortable than saying no. We may be flattered by being asked to do something, or we want to be liked. We frequently find ourselves saying yes to particular individuals over and over again because we dislike confrontation, we don't want to hurt them, or we need their acceptance. Breaking the habit of saying yes is a basic requirement for learning to say no.

• Think before saying yes. Instead of responding on the spot, evaluate your motives and determine why you are saying yes. Use Berry's PIC plan to evaluate each request made of you.

•Prioritize. Pray, asking *Is it God's will?*

•Investigate. Ask, *What will it cost in terms of time, effort, and progress toward my goals?*

•Consult your calendar, asking how this fits with other plans and responsibilities.

• Make sure others are aware of your time demands. Though I am often irritated by those who act as if I should be at their service because I stay at home, I have learned that I can't expect friends to know my working hours without my communicating my intentions.

• Respect your own time as well as others' time. Don't let others, often complete strangers, establish your priorities. Saying yes to one thing almost always means saying no to something else. What you choose to do with your time is important, for you will be held accountable to the Lord for how you spend it.

• Don't be a "solve it all." Don't get in the habit of saying yes just to solve other people's time problems. Someone else's time problems are not your responsibility.

Learning to Say No

Here are some suggestions of how to say no the right way.

• Don't offer excuses. Just say no nicely and directly. Matthew 5:37 (TLB) concludes, "Say a simple 'Yes I will,' or 'No I won't.'" Do not launch into lengthy explanations. You're not asking for permission to decline; you are saying no.

• Say no with tact and politeness. Use pleasant, persuasive words and be considerate of other people's feelings. When you decline a request, thank the other person for asking you, empathize with them, and offer encouragement. Provide suggestions, new ideas, or other options if appropriate.

• Develop a method of saying no. Develop a specific *no* statement and practice saying it. (I'm going to have to say no this time. That is a wonderful idea, but I am not going to be able to do it.) Choose a statement you are comfortable with so you can say no clearly, kindly, and nonoffensively.

• Stick with the decision you make. Though some may see your saying no as personal rejection, don't give in to the criticism that might result or don't strike back with criticism yourself. Don't feel guilty about saying no. Ask yourself, *What should I feel guilty about? What's wrong with saying no? What are my priorities? What is God's will for me?* Remember, saying no may be God's will!

The biggest challenge facing Christian leaders is not separating the good from the bad, but taking the best out of all the good. We need to learn, usually the hard way, that we must say no to some things that we really want to do in order to say yes to the very best things. A song by Gloria Gaither titled "Yes to Something Higher" reiterates this belief: "When you sense a calling that is the best that is within you, When you know deep in your heart you've found a better way, Turn your back on all the voices that would drag you downward; Saying 'no' may be the grandest 'yes' you'll ever say."

Following Christ does not mean doing everything others want you to do. Instead, it means discerning in your heart what God has called you to do and saying no to what you haven't been called to do.

MAKE THE TIME

Think about some of the relationships or types of situations where you have said yes inappropriately recently. Ask yourself:
1. What were my motives for saying yes? Was I trying to please someone? Was I worried about the other person's feelings?

_____
_____
_____

2. To whom do you most often say yes when you need to say no? When is this problem most likely to occur? Are you more apt to say yes if you are approached while you are very busy or in the middle of something else? _____
_____

43

3. Put together a plan of action for preventing this from happening next time. Prepare for the occasion.

_____

_____

4. Practice your new response. Develop some specific *no* statements for several situations (uninvited callers, when asked to do something, when asked to assume a position).

_____

_____

Delegating Your Work

Everyone knows that one way of saving time is to let Jane do it (as long as your name is not Jane). The idea that a good manager gets things done through others has been around for a long time. Examples of delegation are found in the Bible.

Moses is a good example of someone who was filling his time doing good things, yet not accomplishing the God-given tasks before him. It took his father-in-law, Jethro, to point out, "You cannot handle it alone" (Ex. 18:18). Jethro focused Moses on his main responsibilities and proposed that the remaining tasks be done by others (vv. 20-23). This incident sets the classic biblical precedent for delegation as a way of controlling one's time.

Jesus made use of this management skill. When sending out the disciples, He practiced the basic principles of training others. Mark 6 illustrates that Jesus taught and demonstrated what He wanted the disciples to do, sent them out to do it, and provided time for evaluation and encouragement.

Reasons for Not Delegating

Why do we find it so hard to delegate? Several rationales come to mind.

• We think that if we don't do it, no one will. I especially find myself thinking this when it comes to church work. I must be like the prophet Elijah who ran to God saying, "Oh I'm the only one who cares or is doing anything." At those times God must remind me as He did the Old Testament prophet, "There are seven thousand others . . . " (1 Kings 19:14-18).

• We have the attitude that no one can do it as well as us. Thinking we are indispensable is a form of false pride that encourages us to waste time.

• We sometimes fear that relinquishing responsibilities means giving up authority or control. Though I want my son to become a responsible adult, there are some responsibilities that I just can't bring myself to turn over to him. Part of me wants to keep him forever "my baby," to protect him, and I must admit, also to control him.

• We may be hesitant to delegate because if someone learns to do the task without our assistance we may not feel needed anymore. Or what if they can do it better than us? We fear the possibility of losing status or being replaced. In actuality, another's success in a delegated role should be a positive reflection on our ability to manage. And whatever the team—a family, business, church, or organization—everyone benefits from the progress of individual team members.

• My greatest rationale for not delegating is the belief that delegating is an admission of failure or inadequacy. We get this twisted picture that delegating responsibilities means neglecting part of our responsibility or our role. The truth is, as we learn to delegate we are given more time to dedicate to those relationships and responsibilities that are most important to us.

• We often fear that delegating is an imposition on others who are just as busy as we are. We do need to be considerate of others and their responsibilities. Be careful not to save the easy tasks for yourself and give away the dirty work. Be willing to carry your part of the load. But on the other hand, evaluate the situation thoughtfully. Are there others who can help carry the load? Are there family members who need to share the responsibility? Is there an individual who would view a certain task that you consider a chore to be a "piece of cake"? Or is there someone you are denying a blessing of service or sense of accomplishment by your refusing to delegate?

• It takes too much time to delegate. How often have you said, *It's just easier or quicker to do it myself?* In some situations this may actually be the case. Taking time to train and guide others is time well invested.

Help in Delegating

Though we know its value, delegating is one of those time management tools that is difficult to implement because we often are not sure when to do so. Try this good rule of thumb: delegate the things you can't do, the things that others can do better or with greater ease, or the things that are not a part of your primary goals or tasks.

When we finally decide that delegating is a necessary time-saving device, the following suggestions may help make it an easier tool to use.

• Learn to ask for help. Often we seem so efficient that others do not realize how burdensome our time loads are. Berry notes that there are two ways to ask for help. One is the silent, indirect method; the other, the direct approach. In using the indirect method, let the need speak for itself. If you feel overburdened with tasks, try cutting back on the quantity of your work. This is an effective way to ask for help.

Another method is to use the direct approach. Remember, people are not mind readers. Often they do not know we need help unless we ask. And we are often hesitant to ask because doing so seems to be a sign of weakness. Saying you need help is another effective way to delegate duties.

• When you ask for help, make sure the individual understands exactly what you want, but don't impose your methods. Don't fall into the my-way-or-not-at-all trap. Sometimes we are more concerned with the process than the progress. While this is a desirable concern in some situations, the end result should be our focus when we are seeking more time through delegation.

• Delegate the tasks that you don't do well or that are hard for you. Unless you are personally responsible for a task or are performing a certain duty as a learning experience, don't waste time doing something that someone else can do better or would enjoy more. By delegating you may be giving someone else the opportunity to utilize their gifts or talents.

• Delegate both responsibility and authority. When we ask someone to help but fail to give them the necessary authority to make decisions, they often loose interest and drop out. On several occasions I have enlisted help with our youth program at church, only to find that in a few weeks, I am back to running a one-woman show. I failed to challenge the volunteers by giving them major responsibilities or the needed authority to step out on their own. Consequently, they claimed no sense of ownership in the program and often felt unneeded or as if they were wasting their time.

• The flip side of this principle is also true. Even though you have delegated a task, you are ultimately responsible. That is

why training is a crucial part of delegating. When we ask someone to assume a certain aspect of our job responsibilities it is
important that we give all the necessary information, remain
available for questions, assist when needed, and offer praise
and credit for a job well done.

• Be considerate. Do not unload responsibility and then walk
away. When you ask for help, give specific directions. Be willing
to take time to show someone how to do something, then follow
up when necessary. Do not dump all the dirty work onto others
and save the best or easiest jobs for yourself. Try to assign
tasks that relate to a person's interests and talents whenever
possible and rotate the less pleasant ones. Be eager to offer
encouragement and praise and give appropriate credit to the
delegatee.

Delegating is time-consuming. One has to be organized
enough to know what needs to be done. It often takes more
time to explain, instruct, and follow up than to do a task yourself. Though it is a tough discipline to master, delegation has a
double payoff. Both you and the delegatee can benefit. The delegatee learns basic skills, develops talents, and shares ownership in a project. While sometimes we want to say, *I can do it
better or faster*, delegating saves time in the long run, freeing
your time for more important matters.

MAKE THE TIME

1. What are reasons you have a hard time delegating?

_____

_____

2. List specific situations where you find it difficult to delegate.

_____

_____

3. Choose one area where you need to delegate. Which of the
hints offered in this chapter would be most helpful to you?

_____

_____

_____

47

CHAPTER SEVEN

I'll Get Around to It—Tomorrow

On with it, then, and finish the job! Be as eager to finish it as you were to plan it (2 Cor. 8:11 TEV).

If only I could receive credit for my good intentions! So often our spirits are willing but our actions lag far behind. Procrastination! I sometimes wonder if even Paul himself didn't experience similar challenges. He wrote, "Though the will to do good is there, the deed is not. The good which I want to do, I fail to do" (Rom. 7:18 NEB).

Procrastination is the art of postponing things, putting them off until the last minute, then rushing to finish them and sometimes not getting them done at all. For some, it is the continued avoidance of starting a task and seeing it to its conclusion. For others, it is a matter of doing easier, low-priority chores instead of more difficult, high-priority tasks. In our efforts to become more like the Master Manager we must gain control of our time by learning to deal with procrastination.

Confessions of a Procrastinator

Unfortunately, I am not known for getting things done ahead of time, and the personal examples of my own procrastination are numerous. Spending sleepless nights as a student, finishing papers, and cramming for exams at the last minute. Scurrying around on December 23 (or even the 24th) to take care of last-minute Christmas shopping. Watching the stack of junk on the basement floor grow to insurmountable proportions as it awaits spring (ha) cleaning.

My most vivid personal example of procrastination revolves

around the birth of my first child, Logan. Early in my pregnancy, a good friend Keri (Mrs. Do-it-ahead-of-time) encouraged me to begin making preparations for the child's birth. "Have you found a baby book?" "What about birth announcements?" "Let's go pick out nursery furnishings." (She was expecting her second child). "Go on and wash those blankets and sleepers so they will be ready. You don't want to be rushed at the last minute, and you won't feel like doing much later on anyway."

Her prodding questions and encouraging suggestions had little effect. I dreamed and planned and shopped but made little concrete effort toward actually getting ready. I guess I wanted the experience of being pregnant, of planning for our first child, and dreaming about the future to last awhile longer.

Well, to make a long story short, Logan arrived while we were vacationing, 700 miles from home, two-and-a-half months early. For the next month, as he grew and gained strength in a neonatal intensive care unit, I took care of the neglected arrangements . . . ordering announcements and buying a baby book, picking out wallpaper, calling in paint colors to the hardware store at home, and sewing bedroom accessories. I even supervised (from long distance) nursery preparations that were graciously being made by awaiting friends at home. When Logan and I did finally arrive home, four weeks later, he had to sleep in the hall on the floor because the smell of fresh paint was too strong and a bed still hadn't been purchased.

Why Do We Procrastinate?

We've all done it—around tax time, when the kitchen floor needs waxing, when it's time for routine medical exams. It is human nature to want to avoid things that are difficult, painful, or dull. But for some people, procrastination is more than a bad habit. It is an almost paralyzing way of life. Let's take a look at some of the causes of procrastination.

Delaying Out of Fear

Jane Burka and Lenora Yuen, who spent a bulk of their professional lives working with chronic procrastinators, wrote an excellent resource on understanding and overcoming the problem (*Procrastination: Why You Do It, What to Do About It*). The authors conclude that while one may be tempted to label the procrastinator as lazy, disorganized, or just plain ornery, the root of the behavior is often fear of failure, success, being controlled, becoming separate from others, or being too attached. Let's look at these inappropriate fears.

1. Fear of failure

Many procrastinators fear being judged by others or are too hard on themselves. They are afraid they will be found lacking and that even their best efforts won't be good enough.

These people feel their worth depends solely on how well they perform. Notorious perfectionists, they do not want to try anything until they know exactly how everything will work. If there is any possibility of failure or malfunction, the perfectionist resists taking action. She wants no one to see the chink in her armor, so therefore, she procrastinates to prevent the possibility of potential problems. Ironically, when the procrastinator finally moves, there is no hope of doing an outstanding job and this is precisely why the procrastinator waited so long: so she can preserve the idealized illusions about herself. Had she given herself enough time and still done a mediocre job she would have had to face the fact that her best efforts were not good enough (by her own impossible standards, anyway). By her delay the procrastinator avoids disappointing herself by falling short of her goals.

2. Fear of success

Other procrastinators worry about what will happen if they do manage to do a first-class job. If you find yourself slowing down on a project that is going well or if you panic when you receive recognition, you may be suffering from this fear, rooted in the mistaken notion that success can only bring trouble. Procrastinators who fear success often feel guilty for winning. They fear that others will resent their success or that it might hurt their feelings. Some procrastinators fear that success might put them in the spotlight where they will be vulnerable to criticism or abuse. Others procrastinate out of fear that success might leave them no time for relaxation. These delayers conclude that if they begin early, they will use all the time available on the project but if they delay, they can get the project done in less time and the unused time can be spent at will.

3. Fear of being controlled

Many procrastinate because they want to feel they are in control. Procrastination is a way of saying, *You can't make me do this.* Just as a child stalls to get back at overbearing parents, we stall to prove a point or make a statement to a demanding spouse, critical boss, or dogmatic friend. In this situation a procrastinator's self-worth is based on her not conforming.

4. Fear of separation

For some, procrastination is a way of maintaining closeness with others. They put things off, do poorly, and ask for endless advice as a tool for keeping others attached to them. Some delay in order to maintain or begin a dependent relationship with someone, or establish an environment they hope will take care of them. For example, students may postpone finishing college because they do not want to leave the secure university setting. A divorced woman may procrastinate on all her financial matters because doing it herself means admitting that she is really on her own. By digging themselves into a deep hole, many procrastinators conclude that someone is bound to come get them out.

5. Fear of attachment

For others, procrastination serves as a means of keeping people away or at a safe distance, protecting them from intimate relationships. No one wants to get involved with someone whose life seems to always be on the brink of disaster, someone with outstanding debts, a rundown car, a messy house. You can postpone calling friends for a Saturday night get-together until everyone has already made plans. It may look as if you have tried to be sociable, but actually you end up with an evening to yourself and are more relieved than sorry.

Other fears that lead to procrastination are confrontation, the unknown, and facing reality. Acts gives an account of procrastination resulting from fear as Felix, the governor of Judea, reacted to Paul: "Several days later Felix came with his wife Drusilla, who was a Jewess. He sent for Paul and listened to him as he spoke about faith in Christ Jesus. As Paul discoursed on righteousness, self-control and the judgment to come, Felix was afraid and said, 'That's enough for now! You may leave. When I find it convenient, I will send for you'" (Acts 24:24-25).

Other Reasons for Delaying

Aside from fears, there are other reasons for procrastination.

1. Lack of direction and clear plans prevent many from taking positive action. My husband is not much of a handyman and will find any excuse to get out of fixing a problem around the house. He usually procrastinates because he does not know what to do or how to start.

2. Some find that putting things off may gain them attention. Unfortunately there is little recognition for the one who quietly gets a job done on time. The procrastinator may find negative attention preferable to being ignored or overlooked.

3. Another interesting cause of procrastination among Christians is spiritualizing decision making. "When the Spirit moves, I'll get started." "After I've prayed for several weeks, then I'll begin working on the task." "If God wants it to work out, He'll make it happen. He doesn't need me." While waiting for God's leadership is vital, there are some aspects of His will that need no mystical translation.

4. Some procrastinate as a result of parental influence. Through parents who regularly completed our unfinished chores we learn that nothing serious happens when we postpone our work. Someone will take up the slack. A perfectionist-type procrastinator probably had parents who continually admonished, "If it is worth doing at all, it is worth doing well."

5. Rick Yohn, in *Finding Time*, reminds us that overscheduling of personal responsibilities and failure to prioritize often forces one to resort to procrastination. Have you ever turned on the microwave and the vacuum cleaner at the same time and found yourself suddenly without power? That's overload. If the circuits in your house are pushed to their limit, the circuit breaker trips, and the electricity goes out.

People can overload, too. They spend their energies in so many directions that their circuit blows, leading to anger, frustration, stress, and depression. The body can't help but say: "Stop! That's enough, I can't take any more!" A person who is overloaded looses the desire to take any action at all.

6. Some people, operating on the assumption that they work best under pressure, develop a wait-to-the-last-minute style for everything they do. Over the years they have trained themselves to get the adrenaline pumping as the deadline approaches. Just as some get a thrill from driving race cars, playing the stock market, or bungee jumping, others actually enjoy the sense of risk that comes from delaying until the last possible minute. These people often experience health problems that result from the stress and pressure. Also, strained relationships with family members, co-workers, and friends occur as the postponer, like a bulldozer, mows over everything that stands in the way in an attempt to complete the task.

7. Another cause of procrastination is failure to distinguish between the urgent and the important. Because we get caught up in the daily demands of life we often neglect what is really essential. These important matters do not cry out for attention as loudly as those urgent demands and thus are more easily put off and neglected, until often it is too late (see chapter six).

Confronting Procrastination

Putting off what has to be done really doesn't make sense. Ignoring obligations and responsibilities does not make them go away. The dishes you left in the sink will still be there in the morning. Procrastinating usually compounds the situation, leaving a monumental task instead of a simple chore. And while thinking up ways to put off doing something may provide a temporary "holiday," it often takes as much time, effort, and creativity as does facing up to the job and getting it done.

One Step at a Time

There is no easy cure for procrastination, but the first step is to convince yourself of the need for a change. Look at what your habit has cost you—lowered self-confidence, strained relationships, feelings of anxiety, guilt, resentment, stress, and despair (not to mention loss of possible job advancement, recognition, respect, etc.). Once you have decided to stop procrastinating, modify your behavior.

1. Analyze your procrastination history. Write down two or three times when you've procrastinated in the past. Describe the circumstances and try to identify the motive. Think about when you are most likely to procrastinate at work, at school, at home. What do you do instead of the task at hand? Clean your desk, raid the refrigerator, call a friend, take a nap? Keep a record of excuses you make. Try to get a clear picture of your particular brand of procrastination. This will help you prepare yourself to procrastinate less the next time.

2. Make a list of all the tasks you tend to put off. Then prioritize that list from the most to the least important. Can some of these tasks be delegated? Can some be dropped? Can you trade an unwanted task for your help to another person?

3. Set reasonable, reachable goals—goals that are specific and concrete. Break big jobs into manageable chunks then do them one by one. Instead of trying to clean your entire office, clean out your top desk drawer, sort through the mail pile, or file the materials on top of your desk.

4. Visualize the benefits of completing your project—sparkling windows, a restored friendship, loose fitting jeans. Promise yourself a reward and follow through when your goal has been achieved. Don't wait for praise from others (it may never come), but reward yourself for a job well done.

5. Enlist the support of others as you battle procrastination. Tell someone what you are working on and when you want to complete it. If you know someone with a goal similar to yours, like losing weight or exercising regularly, make a plan together. Call each other for support when you are tempted to quit or need help getting unstuck.

6. Because stress is a constant companion to the chronic procrastinator, learn to relax. Learn to be calm when you feel yourself tensing, rushing, panicking. Use scheduled time for leisure and recreation, not as another delaying tactic, but to energize you to action.

7. Utilize the fact that energy levels vary throughout the day. If

you are a morning person, schedule work on your tough, important jobs during your prime time. Schedule easier tasks when you are less attentive.

8. Make an "unschedule" of your already-committed activities. One major mistake procrastinators make is being unrealistic about time. They plan too much, overestimate the time they have available, and underestimate the time it takes to do a job. By preparing an "unschedule," the procrastinator can clearly see how much time is already spoken for.

Do this by keeping a schedule of daily activities. First put in all the things you are already committed to doing or what you think you might be doing. Then look at what uncommitted time you have left. This is all the time you have available to work on a given project. Do you need to free yourself of some commitments? Do changes need to take place to provide more time in your schedule?

9. Use even little bits of time. Often procrastinators never start a project because they insist on having the full amount of time it will take to complete the project stretched out before them. One rarely has several hours free all at once, but everyone can find 15 minutes or half-an-hour here and there. It is amazing how much can be done in a few short bits of time.

The Swiss Cheese Method

Alan Lakein, in *How to Get Control of Your Life and Your Time*, suggests using the Swiss Cheese Method to get yourself started on one of those difficult tasks that you keep putting off. By accomplishing several easy five-minute tasks (he calls them *instant tasks*) that are related to the larger project, you have a system of poking holes in the overwhelming job and can gain momentum for really getting started.

One nice thing about the Swiss Cheese Method is that it doesn't really matter what instant task you select as long as it's easy (the easier the better) and related to the overwhelming project. How much of a contribution the particular instant task makes is far less important than the overriding objective of the moment: to do something—anything—on the biggie!

Ask Lakcin's Question

A related time management tool for dealing with procrastination is to ask yourself, *What is the best use of my time, right now?* In professional circles this is referred to as "Lakein's question," named for Alan Lakein who devised the planning tool. Lakein suggests asking yourself this question all through the day, particularly if you are not positive about whether you are using your time to your best advantage. Ask it when you complete a task or are at a natural transition, when you have been interrupted by a visitor or a phone call, or when you are torn between two different projects. Ask, *What is the best use of my time, right now?* when you notice that you have become distracted, when you detect a tendency to procrastinate, or when you are running out of steam. Hang a poster with Lakein's question in your office, on a bulletin board, in your notebook, or on your refrigerator as a reminder to keep asking yourself whether you are using your time to your best advantage.

If you struggle with procrastination, you are not alone. How often have we echoed Apostle Paul's apparent self-reproach as he wrote to the Romans, "I do not understand what I do. For what I want to do I do not do" (Rom. 7:15). We cannot easily transform the bad habits of procrastination that took years to acquire. But by thoughtful analysis of the reasons for our postponing we can alter our attitude toward the problem. And changed attitudes become a springboard for modified behavior. We procrastinators with good intentions would do well to adhere to the challenge of the Apostle Paul in another letter: "On with it, then, and finish the job! Be as eager to finish it as you were to plan it" (2 Cor. 8:11 TEV).

MAKE THE TIME

Look again at the suggestions for confronting procrastination and apply them, step by step, to a particular task that you are having difficulty completing.

_____

_____

56

CHAPTER EIGHT

Redeeming the Time

Walk in wisdom toward them that are without,
redeeming the time (Col. 4:5 KJV).

Do you ever feel like you are loosing time? Time leaks are those minutes and seconds we inadvertently let slip from our lives. Like gas leaks in a house, they are difficult to locate and so small they often seem irrelevant. However, if they aren't traced and stopped, they are costly. Jesus was a master at getting the most out of His time. Just as the early Christians were urged to redeem their time, we too must learn new ways to grab hold of the fleeting moments and make the most of them.

Capitalize on Your Idle Time

Idle time is when the engine is running but you are actually going no where . . . time when the clock is ticking, but nothing is happening. This used to be the most frustrating time for me. I would anxiously flip magazine pages in the waiting room. I would stand in line at the checkout counter, patting my foot as if the constant motion would speed things up. When I saw a traffic congestion, I would maneuver around parking lots and store entrances in an effort to not be caught by a light or left waiting in the car.

It was a wonder that I had not contracted some mysterious wrist ailment as a result of constantly checking my watch, watching the precious moments tick by as I stood idly in line or waited impatiently in my car. There must be something to do with those inevitable gaps of inactivity.

I have since learned several helpful recommendations for making progress during idle time.

1. Take something to do when you go somewhere for those just-in-case times. Whether you find yourself waiting at the doctor's office or arriving early to pick up children from school, be prepared to use the unexpected idle time wisely. Write a thank-you note, hem a skirt, or plan your weekly menu.

2. If you have regular idle time, such as commuting, plan ways to use that time. Pray, listen to tapes, plan your day, think through a problem, plan a project. I did a lot of commuting to seminary and often found that I couldn't wait to get to my car so I could have "my time" alone, to think, pray, dream, and plan. Make those minutes that many consider a waste of time a profitable part of your day.

3. Eliminate as much idle time as possible. Make appointments when plausible. Call ahead to confirm your appointment and to see if you will be seen on schedule. Plan your errands so they can be done on your way to another stop. When possible, choose times with less congestion and fewer people.

4. Consolidate your time. Many of us do more than one thing at a time out of necessity, but often it helps to plan ahead how you might accomplish as much as possible. Keep a basket of items to be mended and sewing supplies by the telephone. Keep stationery or ironing by the television. I cut out coupons while on lengthy car rides and keep a little bag of smocking packed and ready to grab if I go somewhere and know I might spend time waiting. Make a list of all the things you can do at the same time, then get set up to take advantage of the opportunities.

One word of caution: be careful not to offend others or devalue precious family time. My husband frequently says to me, "Do you always have to be doing something?" I continually remind myself that it really is OK to sit down and watch a movie with my husband (without a project in my hands) or to stop what I'm doing to color with my preschooler. There are times when friends and family members should be given more than my physical presence.

5. Keep a list of ten-minute jobs, projects that can be done in ten minutes or less. Post it on a bulletin board. Everyday, make a list of specific tasks. This can be done at home as well as in the office. For example:

empty the dishwasher
put a load of clothes on to wash
fold and put away a load of clothes
clean off the coffee table
write a postcard
sew on a button
clean out my purse
water the plants
make a phone call.

It is amazing how many times during the day you find yourself with an extra ten minutes, and how many things you can do in ten minutes. Those annoying little jobs that mount up can disappear quickly if you attack them one at a time.

MAKE THE TIME

1. Think about periods of idle time in your day. What can you do to redeem this time? _____

_____

2. Make a list of standard ten-minute jobs for work and home; post it in a visible place. _____

_____

Refrain from Hurry

The Queen in *Alice in Wonderland* said: "It takes all the running you can do to stay in place. If you want to get someplace else, you must run twice as fast as that." The old saying that "haste makes waste" is so true. When we hurry, we make mistakes that claim more time than if we hadn't rushed. It has been said that one of the great disadvantages of hurry is that it takes such a long time. Can you verify that statement with personal experience? Have you ever tried to take a shortcut to avoid a traffic problem and ended up getting lost? Burned the cookies because you turned up the temperature to try to cook them a little quicker? How often have you run out the door, late for a meeting, only to return to the house three times to retrieve forgotten items, before you even get down the driveway?

Hurry is counterproductive, decreasing one's efficiency as well as enjoyment. In *When I Relax, I Feel Guilty*, Tim Hansel says that hurry may be one of the greatest sins of our age.

The world is dizzy with hurry, overwhelmed with a desire to precipitate the future. Often, we overlook the important things because of our desire to make things happen. We no longer participate in the simple delights of the earth. So how do we keep from hurrying? The following suggestions may be helpful if you constantly feeling rushed.

Adjust Your Schedule

Don't keep such a tight schedule that you are always pressed for time. You do not have to be busy every minute of the day. Cramming your day with activity is not redeeming the time; rather, it is gulping it down.

Instead, try to savor life, as you would relish every bite of a gourmet meal. Immerse yourself in the simple delights of every day—the morning breeze in your face, moist grass beneath your feet, the smell of honeysuckle in the evening, a child in your arms.

Get a head start. To cover unforeseen interruptions, plan on arriving ten minutes before a scheduled activity. If something unexpected comes up, you can deal with it briefly and still avoid a last-minute rush.

Deal Constructively with Interruptions

It never fails. You have 20 minutes to make a 15-minute trip across town for a meeting and your car won't start. You've set the day aside to shop for groceries and run errands and the school calls saying you need to pick up a sick child. Dinner guest are to arrive in 90 minutes and a "long-lost" friend appears at your front door.

Interruptions! Around our house, we have a standing truth, just about as reliable as the law of gravity. Lloyd's law says you can count on being up all night with a baby who is screaming with an apparent ear infection only if you have a million things to do tomorrow. The more you plan and the more focused you seem to be about accomplishing your tasks, the more annoying interruptions can be.

Often, when we take the time to evaluate the nature and frequency of interruptions, we realize that we can do something about them. Notice whether your interruptions occur regularly or in any sort of pattern. Interruptions often result because of a breakdown in communication. For example, your lonely neighbor calls just about every morning with some problem. Could it be that she is not aware you have established office hours at home? Or a co-worker consistently stops by your desk to ask your opinion on a project. Maybe she does not understand her assignment and needs further instruction.

Frequent interruptions may also signal bad timing on your part. Your children are constantly interrupting in the afternoons when you like to make bread. Maybe you should consider baking while they are at school.

Handle Simple Interruptions

Simple interruptions from callers or unexpected guests (those of the noncrisis nature) can be handled in several ways. Take the direct approach when it comes to informing others about your time demands. A considerate individual will appreciate your honesty, and an explanation will clarify your possible lack of attention or preoccupation.

Add a dash of diplomacy to avoid running the risk of hurt feelings. Keep in mind that sometimes you are the interruptor for another person. Remember the Golden Rule! Be positive and when possible, indicate when you will have a more free moment. This verifies your interest and also reduces the risk of misunderstanding. For example, instead of saying, "I only have 15 minutes, Mom," try, "Oh, this is great, Mom. I have 15 minutes before my next commitment. I'm glad you called." Or, to the co-worker who drops by during her break say, "I'd love to hear all about your new house. But right now, I'm so distracted by this noon deadline that is coming up, it is hard to concentrate on anything else. Let's get together for lunch tomorrow so you can tell me all the details."

Another suggestion for dealing with unexpected callers is to find out what the real need is. A simple direct response may be all that is necessary. If the need can be met later, pull out an appointment calendar and make the date right then.

If you need to bring a conversation to a close, indicate your intentions with appropriate body movements. Stand or move toward the door. Indicate to your caller that your time is gone by a touch of the hand. If you regularly find it difficult to close a conversation yourself, ask a spouse, secretary or co-worker to assist by announcing in the presence of the visitor that it is time for your next commitment.

See Interruptions as Opportunities

There are times when interruptions should be treated as opportunities. Jesus accomplished His purpose and never appeared to be without time for unscheduled interruptions. In one Biblical example He was on His way to see Jairus' sick daughter. He must have been focused on His goal, arriving before the sick girl died. But Jesus was interrupted by another one in need . . . not a ruler's child at the point of death, but an unclean, chronically ill woman. Jesus lovingly and patiently took the time to heal the woman and to bless her. He turned the interruption into an opportunity.

In *The Time Minder*, Ruth Miller says that interruptions can be viewed in one of two ways: either as annoying, frustrating blockades to our best–laid plans or as God's little nudges. Similarly, Charles W. Shedd in *Time for All Things* refers to "divine interruptions." He concludes that one of the marks of Christian greatness is a certain "interruptability." Our life should have an elastic quality with room for one more real need if it comes from higher up. Certainly, the parable of the Good Samaritan is a poignant reminder of a Christian's responsibility to respond redemptively to interruptions. The Phillips translation of James 1:2 admonishes us to rejoice in trials and tribulations, not resenting them as intruders but welcoming them as friends. (Looks like I'll never be at a loss for companionship!)

Deal Redemptively with Interruptions

Several steps can be taken to deal redemptively with interruptions. Shedd suggests planning one's schedule with a stretch factor, disciplining one's self in the art of early starts and before-deadline finishes. Having committed your schedule to God at the beginning of the day, look carefully at each interruption, asking God, "What is it You want me to learn from this, or how do You want me to respond to this, Father?"

A word of caution: Miller reminds us that not all interruptions come from God. Some arrive special delivery, designed to discourage and distract. But we can turn these, too, into victories, by offering them to God, asking Him to use them. Our refusal to grow irritable over interruptions is a victory. Although interruptions play havoc with the best made plans, there is always enough time to do what Jesus calls us to do. Our generous God more than makes up for time we give away.

An old proverb reminds us that "man's interruptions are God's opportunities." As seekers of the kingdom we must be attuned to the truth that on numerous occasions, the interrupter is more important than the interrupted. There are times when, just as the Master Manager, we must say yes to what looks like the moment for a justified no.

MAKE THE TIME
1. Look back at your interruptions over the last few days. Is there a pattern? When did they occur?

_____

_____

2. Recall a "divine" interruption in your life.

_____

_____

Counter Distractibility

8:05 A.M. Alone at last. I return to the kitchen, newspaper in hand, for a few solitary moments. I pour a cup of coffee and pop a slice of bread in the toaster. While it is cooking I decide to load the dishwasher. As I go to the table to get my son's cereal bowl I see his Sunday sport coat on the chair. While returning his coat to his room, I decide to take a few minutes to straighten his closet. While there, I pack up a bag of too-small items to deliver to a neighbor. I take them to the kitchen door and there remember my now-cold toast.

I push the toaster down to quickly rewarm the toast and while I'm waiting, wipe the counter top. I stop to sort through a stack of mail, and finding a bill that should have been paid yesterday, go to the bedroom to get my purse. On the way, I straighten the pillows on the sofa, stack the newspapers on the coffee table and pick up two pairs of dirty socks. I drop them in the clothes hamper in the bathroom and notice that there is toothpaste all over the sink.

After wiping the sink, I replace the empty toilet paper roll, straighten the towels, and return the baby doll to her appropriate resting place. Stacking a few books on the toy shelf, I notice a dirty juice cup in the corner. Returning it to the kitchen, I see the unpaid bill on the counter, the yet-to-be loaded dishwasher and the cold-again toast. I throw the toast in the garbage and notice that the trash can needs emptying . . .

Busy people often suffer from the disease of distractibility. We see so many unfinished projects and so many tasks that need to be done that we are easily distracted. Even though we get a lot of little things done, we jump from one task to another and never have a real feeling of completion. We still have so much to do that what we have done pales in significance to what is always yet to be done.

Those who have the "pinball syndrome," bouncing from task to task, must learn to not be so hard on themselves. If you stop and take stock, you will see that you really have accomplished quite a bit. Even so, here is a rule for staying focused on our tasks: have a schedule; have a system; keep it simple.

Whether you are performing routine household chores, managing an office, or operating a multi-million dollar business, there is something about establishing a routine that saves everyone time. Having a schedule assures you that eventually you'll get everything done. It keeps you from stopping in the middle of one job to start another that you notice needs doing. I can stop feeling guilty about the overflowing junk drawer in the kitchen because it is on the list for Friday. Scheduling routine tasks brings a sense of order and commits you to completing a task at a certain time.

We can find a great sense of control when there is a system for doing these recurring tasks. When you repeat a task over and over in the same way, you both conserve and generate energy. You don't have to waste time deciding how to do something. Also, in developing a mental and physical rhythm, habit takes over, freeing your mind to do other things as well. Develop your own system for doing such tasks as applying makeup, doing laundry, cleaning the house, preparing a meal, and handling mail. This is a concrete way to follow the scriptural command to "make the most of every opportunity."

Ruth Miller suggests these questions to help simplify your system: Is there a faster way to do this? Does this task need doing at all? Could someone else do it as well or better? Can it be postponed until a better time? By modifying old habits and eliminating unnecessary steps you can streamline routine tasks, thus freeing more time for more worthwhile pursuits.

Simplify and Organize

You can do a better job of redeeming your time if you will develop two simple habits: simplify your life and get organized.

Simplify Your Life

I must admit that I am a cluttered person . . . a pack rat. I came by this trait naturally—it must be in my blood. My father thinks it's sinful to throw anything away. You name it, he saves it. He's proud to know that I carry on that tradition. Here are some suggestions for moving toward more clutter-free living.

Before buying anything, ask yourself, *Do I really need this? How often will I use it? What do I already own that I could use instead? Is it worth the space it will take up? Will I have to buy anything else to go with it?*

Once a month go through each room of your house looking for anything that can be thrown away; anything not used that can be stored or given away; anything seasonal that should be put away; anything that doesn't serve a purpose anymore.

I am far from being reformed but I do see the value in simplifying life. I am learning that every step toward simplification gives me more time and helps me make everyday decisions more quickly.

Organize

Because I save everything, most of the time I can't find anything. A good deal of my time goes toward trying to find the item that I put someplace so that I would remember where it was when I started looking for it. I know it's here somewhere.

Organizing helps you make fewer decisions. Putting bills in a special box means never again having to worry about where you put them, or forgetting to pay them. Organizing baking goods, canned goods, and prepared boxed meals means that your children or spouse can help put away groceries or prepare a meal because there is a system everyone understands.

While most people are not naturally organized, they find that getting organized ultimately takes less time and energy than dealing with chaos every day. Files, bins, and drawer dividers are inexpensive ways to help find more time for the important things in life.

Listen to Your Body

Our bodies can tell us a good deal about wise use of our time. Each of us have varying levels of efficiency throughout the day. Are you more alert and productive early or late in the day? There was a time in my life (in my younger days) when it seemed that I never really got rolling until late in the evening, and then between 10:00 P.M and 1:00 A.M. I really got things accomplished. Notice when you do your best work. If you tend to drag toward the end of the day, save the more routine tasks for the afternoon. Focus your energies on high-level tasks during your most productive hours, minimizing the time you normally waste fumbling through projects that tax your mind when you're just not up to them.

Listen to your body. If you are not feeling well, this is not the time to begin a new project. Sometimes it might be best to put at the top of your list for the day: put my feet up, take a bubble bath, read a book, take the day for myself.

MAKE THE TIME

1. What can you do to simplify your life?

_____

_____

2. In what areas of your life do you need to be more organized?

_____

_____

Lessons from Mary and Martha

Often, in the demands of everyday life, we lose sight of our goals and get sidetracked by things that don't really matter. The urgent demands seem to cry out for our immediate response and the most important tasks go unattended. When this happens, God's will becomes fuzzy, like a photograph taken with an improperly focused camera.

Identifying Priorities

Scripture provides an excellent example of how easy it is to have a faulty focus on priorities. Luke records one event. "As Jesus and his disciples were on their way He came to a village where a woman named Martha opened her home to him" (Luke 10:38). Martha must have had the gift of hospitality. She was the one responsible for entertaining the guests, for making them feel welcomed. She must have felt that it was a real privilege that the Lord would choose her home to rest and recuperate. Making her guests comfortable was a priority for her.

"She had a sister called Mary, who sat at the Lord's feet listening to what he said" (v. 39). While Martha was hustling about, Mary chose to listen intently to Jesus' teachings. She wasn't about to pass up an opportunity like this to receive first-hand instruction from the Lord. That was unheard of for a woman in her day. Mary probably was so attuned to His words that she wasn't even aware of what was going on around her.

A Faulty Focus

"But Martha was distracted with all the preparations . . ." (v. 40). Martha must have had a million things to do. She became so wrapped up in what she was doing that her activities distracted her from the Lord. Her focus was faulty; her priorities were out of line.

Sound like anyone you know? I am naturally a Martha, rushing about, filling my day with "doing good," taking pride in my busyness, but sometimes feeling void at the end of the day. Like many of you, I let the everyday hustle and bustle of life distract me from the Lord. All of us, at one time or another, have become so involved in *what* we are doing that we forget *Who* we are doing it for.

The more Martha thought about the situation, the angrier she got and the more self-righteous she felt. She must have said to herself, *This isn't fair. I'm the one who always ends up doing all the work around here.* Finally, Martha could keep silent no longer. She had to say something.

"Lord, don't you care that my sister has left me to do the work by myself? Tell her to help me" (v. 40). Overburdened with responsibility and very frustrated when others didn't seem to appreciate everything she was doing, Martha vented her frustration by condemning others who were not as active. Martha accused Jesus of not caring and before He had a chance to respond, she told Him what to do!

Obviously, Martha had decided that she knew better than the Lord or Mary what her sister's priorities should be. (Ugh, this illustration is getting a bit too personal!) Aren't we a lot like Martha, too? How often do we take it upon ourselves to tell God what is best for us? We judge how others, especially those closest to us, should use their time. We expect their priorities to match ours, and when they don't we feel angry, used, and unappreciated. We criticize what they do when actually our own priorities are the ones out of focus.

Limiting Priorities

Jesus must have chuckled slightly as He lovingly answered Martha's complaint. "Martha, Martha," the Lord answered, "you are worried and upset about many things" (v. 41). Again, we too are like Martha. We waste so much time, energy, and emotions fussing, fuming, and fretting. And the worry makes havoc out of